What Others A

"What a wonderful journey I've just had reading this book. The book is overflowing with so much love, encouragement, wonderful advice, kind words, great exercises and wonderful human stories. I felt so empowered being a woman and fortunate as well. I had a particularly meaningful experience using the breathing techniques one day when I was feeling quite uneasy about something. It helped calm me down and took me to a more relaxed place. It was wonderful. Thank you. Additionally, I loved the women's stories. They were so rich with insight and interest. I know that this book will be a great tool and source of empowerment to so many women."
~ *Marian Hamilton, founder, The Ken Hamilton Caregivers Center, Northern Westchester Hospital, NY*

"I love this book! It is thoughtful, very readable, down-to-earth, and extremely helpful to women at all stages of their lives. In addition to being an eye-opening book and a comfort for individual women, it will be an invaluable resource for coaches and counselors who work with women. The authors have given us a real gift."
~ *Sara B. Hart, PhD, health coach, life coach, and member of worldwide faculty for Time To Think, Inc.*

"*Stand, Flow, Shine: Caring for the Woman Within* is a warm, engaging guide to self-care for women. It is a helpful reminder of the importance of nurturing ourselves, and has practical suggestions for doing so. I highly recommend this lovely book to women committed to living life fully, and with an open heart."
~ *Susanne F. Fincher, art therapist and author of* Creating Mandalas: For Insight, Healing, and Self-Expression

"Judith and Marilyn have created a truly beautiful book filled with great information, practices and insights that assist each of us in being caretakers of our whole Self. As women, taking good care of ourselves is a benefit to everyone around us. This is a guide book to strengthen, support and celebrate all of who we are in our complex lives."
~ *Lucky Sweeny, evolutionary life coach and author of* Conscious Choices, An Evolutionary Woman's Guide to Life

"Brilliant book released with divine timing! In reading the beautiful, powerful words of the authors, we are reminded to take care of our precious body~mind~soul. They shine a light on why we forget about our own self-care. Then, through the sharing of their personal life journeys, Marilyn and Judith gently guide us to open hearted, simple exercises, tools and resources with the wisdom only obtained through experience. Enjoy the book."
~ *Andrea Hylen, founder of Heal My Voice, a non-profit organization offering support to women and girls*

"This book offers a wide variety of helpful ways for women to feel strong, gentle, and connected. The approach of uncovering women's inner strengths and possibilities with different techniques can be used by women from all different cultures and countries. It is wonderful to see how the authors brought together their personal experiences and professional skills in a dedicated and creative way."
~ *Caja Schuurman, psychologist and psychotherapist, Netherlands Area Director of Zonta International, a world-wide women's advocacy organization*

"What a welcome, timely book from two lovely, grounded healers! Take some time to reconnect with your most authentic self with this gentle sweet guidance using nature and story as teacher. Reconnecting with ourselves as women is a gift to all without exception and just what the world needs! Every word, exercise and

narrative is deeply rooted in love, flowing with joy and shining with new possibility for each of us. I feel as if I have been hugged!"
~ *Gina L. Sager, MD. teacher of mindfulness based stress reduction, yoga, and yoga nidra*

"Reading this powerful book has been an insightful and joyful walk through life fully lived. Using natural imagery and personal experience are compelling ways to understand and embrace whatever life teaches us. It is a warm and helpful reminder of how best to use one's self, creativity, and experience to maintain a sense of balance."
~ *Terry Dalsemer, retired psychotherapist and facilitator of support groups for seniors*

"The practices shared in these pages are powerful tools to support living a life of radiance and flow. There is magic in opening to a new way of seeing ourselves; it lives in the opportunity to establish new life-serving practices. When insight and practice come together, it does change everything. Everything. May you shine."
~ *Heather Johnson, associate director, Whidbey Institute for Leadership Transformation, Community Vitality, and Sustainable Action*

"Self-care is a tricky topic in a world where it is still often considered a virtue to put others before self. You must have before you can give and self-care is key. Discipline, at least initially, is required to get that self-care ball rolling and sustained. Both Judith and Marilyn are skilled in a very special kind of way, as mentors; their sincerity vibrates off the pages. This book is a generous offering from two seasoned, soulful, and very humane beings. Thank you!"
~ *Pamela Sackett, Emotion Literacy Advocates' Founding Artist and author of* Speak of the Ghost

STAND
tall like the tree

FLOW
like the river

SHINE
like the sun

Caring for the Woman Within

Judith Waldman and Marilyn F. Clark

Piney Creek Studio

Printed in the United States of America.

ISBN 978-0-9887590-0-8

Published by Piney Creek Studio

For additional copies of
Stand, Flow, Shine: Caring for the Woman Within
or to contact the authors about workshops and speaking engagements, please visit www.StandFlowShine.com or email pineycreekstudio@gmail.com.

Cover design by Lisa Amowitz
Interior design by E. Jusino

Contents

Gratitude

We are so thankful for all the support, help, and caring that we have received on this book-writing journey. We thank our families and many friends who have listened, advised, encouraged, and comforted us along the way.

From Marilyn, to my sweet family: Tamara, Matt, Mike, Susanne, Laura, Joann, Agnes Anne, and dear husband, Bob. My "We Are Going" women's group is a shining treasure on my self-care journey. Thank you Diane, Nancy-Bets, Leah, Lucky, Chris, Susan, Karen, and Sandy. And to so many friends including Jill C., Celia, Georgette, Catherine, Alexia, Margaret, Mary, Jean, Rosemary, and Elaine.

From Judith, to my very dear family and women friends: Bill, Laura, Noah, Eli, Mira, Brook, Anna, Babs, Patty, Linda, Marian, Toby, Gloria, Pat, Maggie, Karan, Greta, Alison, Danute, Jane, Maria, Pamela, Alexandra, Alice, and all the rest of you who checked in regularly on me and the progress of the book. Thank you, every one of you, for all the love and caring that you give me.

We thank our many teachers and mentors who have given so much to us. Most especially, we thank Helen Bonny, Joanna Macy, Gina Sager, Beth Vaughan, and Danute Armstrong.

We are so very grateful for the excellent editing, advising, and hand-holding provided by Gail Burlakoff and Beth Jusino. These two women provided us with an editing education that was invaluable and helped our writing project become a manuscript and now a book.

Beth Jusino, our project manager, helped us through the entire publishing process. We really couldn't have done this without you.

Katherine Burge, copy editor, went over the whole book with her fine-tooth comb and patiently smoothed out the text. Thank you.

Lisa Amowitz, our cover designer, was especially creative and timely. Thanks, Lisa, for getting the tone and feeling of our book.

Our readers, who gave us very useful advice and encouragement, were particularly helpful: Marian Hamilton, Toby Israel, Susan Saunders, Lucky Sweeny, Maggie Hayes, and Sarah Hart.

Ellyn Coe did an excellent job of transcribing the interviews that comprise the "Women's Stories." Thank you, Ellyn.

Thank you to our photographer Bill and the women who grace our photos: Karan Cole, Michelle Stafford, Kirsten Burger, Rebecca DeLibro, Shelly Styker, Rachel Wenck, Emily Grey, Cheri Garber, and little Alexandra.

Each of the women we interviewed inspired and enriched the book in so many ways. Thank you Aisha Dudley Craig, Gloria Shapiro, Joyce Lembhard, Karen Cook, Lena Plummer, Marian Hamilton, Pat Halle, Ray Zwerling, Sarah Golightly, Toby Israel, Mary K. Baxter, Susan Saunders, Tanya Hicks, Josie LaBua, Sophie Fineran, Leah Ulansey, Danute Armstrong, Laura Silver, and Marge Wile.

For her inspiration and grace, we want to single out one of the women we interviewed: Ray. She was 100 years old when

we interviewed her. At 104, she continues to inspire us with her daily practice of reading the *New York Times*, working the *Times* crossword puzzles, and keeping up with her favorite basketball team. She is still very involved with her retirement community where she helps new residents get adjusted.

We especially feel gratitude for each other. We learned that two good friends can also work well together. We blended our writing styles and helped one another clarify what we wanted to communicate to our readers. We negotiated, compromised, and treated each other with love and respect. We also reminded one another to take good care of ourselves throughout the writing process.

Welcome

Hello, dear women. Welcome to this book that we have created for you. Within these pages, you will find many ways to relax, nurture, and empower yourself. With the clear practices suggested in the book, you will learn how self-care can decrease your stress and increase your well-being, bringing you pleasure and joy.

This book will give you resources for now and for the rest of your life. You are embarking on a journey of caring for yourself in new and creative ways. We are pleased to offer support and guidance along the way.

We are experienced psychotherapists who have led self-care workshops for women for over twenty years. We are two women who, for many years, have learned and created tools for our own self-care and for the self-care of other women. We come to this book packed with experience, resources, and women's wisdom. We understand your needs, and we know ways to fill those needs. We offer our expertise and guidance to you.

We stand with you. We celebrate every moment that you wake up to the possibilities of caring for yourself in new ways. Most of all, we know that caring for yourself is a satisfying and rewarding lifetime process. Why not begin now? We encourage you to pack your self-care suitcase and start your journey today.

We hope that you enjoy the journey.

Judith and Marilyn

Stand, Flow, Shine Story

Stand Tall Like the Tree
Flow Like the River
Shine Like the Sun

Judith:

Many of the workshops and retreats that we do are at my place out in the countryside of Maryland. I love the land—the woods, the waters, and the wildlife. Within each workshop plan, there is plenty of time spent outside if the weather allows.

One day I was sitting, alone, on a rock by the stream that runs through our land. I looked up through the branches of a majestic old oak tree and felt the sun shining down on me, and on the water and the tree. I heard the soothing sounds of the stream. I had a feeling of well-being, centeredness, and joy. I had an inspiration for a new way to honor our connection with ourselves and with nature.

Standing on the big rock, I took a step toward the tree, moving my arms up and in the air, and proclaimed, "Stand tall like the tree!" Then, bringing my arms down to chest level, I moved them in a flowing motion and called out, "Flow like the river!" Turning to face the sun, I made a big circular movement with my arms, "Shine like the sun!"

Marilyn and I now use these words and movements in our workshops and retreats as positive affirmations coming from the natural world. We can stand and take in the strength and steadiness of the tree, the soothing flow of the stream, and the warmth and glow of the sun.

 *Stand, Flow, Shine*

⌨ You can follow this movement process and others, as well as relaxation processes and guided meditations, on our website: www.StandFlowShine.com. Look for this symbol throughout the book.

These images—of a tree, a river, and a sun—form our vision and intention for the book you are holding. They embody our strong connection to nature as a replenishing, balancing, and creative force in our lives.

Nature teaches us how to be, how to accept what life gives us, how to adapt to change, and how to care for all of life. Our intention for this book is to help you learn to stand tall, flow, and shine throughout your own life journey.

✍

Marilyn:

We move forward to another place, South Korea, where I traveled with my sister, who had been invited to give lectures and workshops at a hospital. Two young Korean women were wonderful tour guides for us. Over the few days that we were together, we became very fond of one another.

Before the end of the trip, we visited a Korean craft village outside of Seoul. At the calligrapher's booth, I had a sudden inspiration: what fun it would be to give Judith her affirmation in calligraphy: "Stand tall like the tree. Flow like the river. Shine like the sun."

One of the young women helped me negotiate with the calligrapher. As he pulled out his large brushes and set up his paper, the other woman asked me why I wanted these particular words.

I told her about the workshops I did with Judith, how women came to them to have time for themselves and to focus on their lives, their challenges and joys, and what they might need to do to improve their lives. I explained about Judith's movement exercise and described the land where the idea for the exercise was birthed.

Two days later, my sister and I were at the airport with our two Korean guides, who now seemed like daughters. To say good-bye was

difficult and sad because this moment of friendship was soon to become only a memory. As my sister and I passed through the departure gate, we looked back to wave good-bye. The beautiful "daughter" said to me, "Stand tall like a tree. Flow like the river. Shine like the sun!" My heart opened wide in awe of this final, meaningful gesture that connected us as women on our life journeys.

In writing this book, we wanted to record and pass on to other women all that we have learned about how to stand tall, flow, and shine. In our generation, women's place in society and roles in marriage and family were radically changed. The two of us were active in that change. We felt our own strength and the strength of being women in times of exciting change. We learned to stand tall and steady and to feel our roots. We lost and found precious time for ourselves. We discovered wonderful support, nurturing, and wisdom in our women friends. We flowed with the changing face of women in our time. As we came into a stronger sense of who we were as women, we let ourselves shine from the inside out.

Over twenty years ago, on a summer afternoon, we began to talk about all that we had learned personally and professionally about women's self-care. We wanted a way to bring women together to share with one another and to learn new skills. We wanted to offer an opportunity for women to deepen their sense of interconnectedness with themselves, each other, and all of life. From our experience, we knew that when women get together, there is a shared energy and spirit of connection. It was important to us that we help women learn to take better care of themselves by making themselves a priority in their own lives, even as they care for others and the world around them.

Each of us had experience leading groups and facilitating workshops. Marilyn had led workshops, retreats, and training programs in the Bonny Method of Guided Imagery and Music for many years. Judith had been leading therapy groups in her psychotherapy practice. She also facilitated workshops designed by

Interhelp, a national organization based on the Work that Reconnects, created by Joanna Macy. We both brought personal and professional expertise in how to develop self-care practices. Our personal styles complemented one another, and we knew that, together, we could provide women with a sense of being nurtured and safe, along with a workshop program that was informative, well-paced, high energy, and fun. Our journey as workshop leaders together began.

Hundreds of workshops later, we find that while each age group is unique in experiences and concerns, certain needs are common to all women: to give voice to their challenges and joys, to learn to treat themselves with care and compassion, and to find ways to better manage their self-care. Solutions to these needs are the cornerstones of our workshop designs and of this book.

⌀

Judith:

When I look back on this time, I see a richly woven fabric: beautiful settings, hundreds of wonderful women, and a host of workshop experiences. We have provided a journey of intimacy, self-nourishment, poignancy, creativity, and fun. Most of all, we have taught so many women tools and skills with which to take better care of themselves.

Marilyn:

When I look back on this time, I feel smiles, joyfulness, awe, and the unexplainable but palpable energy that is present when women come together to be true to themselves and to share their authentic nature with other women.

⌀

It is our hope that this book will provide you with similar experiences and that you will return to these processes over and over again. Our intention for you is that you feel better connected with yourself and your needs.

As you read and apply good self-care practices, you will feel relaxed, renewed, and empowered. You will learn to prioritize

time for yourself and, thereby, find wonderful support, nurturing, and wisdom within yourself. You will learn to stand tall and steady and to feel your roots like a sturdy tree. You will flow with what life brings you like the soothing flow of the stream. As you come into a stronger sense of who you are, you will relax and deepen into your own being, shining like the sun from the inside out. You will be so glad that you are taking this self-care journey. Now is the best time to begin!

Beginning the Journey

There are so many reasons for you to take good care of yourself. You may be a young woman needing to find ways to calm and empower yourself in the midst of life's complexities. Use these next chapters as a guidebook for your own self-care as you deal with the important decisions that face you now.

Perhaps you are out in the work world where you feel anxious or stressed by the daily demands of your career. Use these ideas to increase your comfort and creativity.

If you are a mother, you are probably juggling many demands every day and rarely taking time to care for your own needs. Use this book as a touchstone and support to help you remember that you need to take care of yourself, too!

At midlife, you might find yourself stretched between the demands of your family and the emerging role of caring for your aging parents. You are aware of your own aging as well. Whether alone, in a relationship, or stretched between generations, you have to find you. Use the following chapters to help you find, redefine, and enjoy who you are becoming in this time of change and transition.

As an elder woman, your physical and mental abilities may be changing, and you are eager to find ways to feel stronger emotionally, mentally, and physically. You also want to feel inner peace at this time of your life. Use this book as a way to find ease, creativity, and relaxation by yourself and with others.

Whoever you are, we provide you with resources to create your own self-care plan. You have the intuitive wisdom to know what you need. Sometimes, though, you may forget what you know, or you may need to learn new ways to take care of yourself.

The following chapters offer processes to help you increase your emotional and physical wisdom and free your creative spirit. We provide exercises for strengthening your ability to use your own resources. And we suggest activities that may help you with a particular need. Some sections will take you to quiet, reflective spaces. Others will bring out a creative zest for living with activities and movement.

We have divided all of the individual activities into three chapters:

"Stand Tall Like the Tree" (Self-Empowerment, Changing Attitude and Behavior)

"Flow Like the River" (Movement and Creative Arts)

"Shine Like the Sun" (Relaxation, Meditation, and Journal Reflections)

Many of these activities can also be adapted for use with a partner or a group of women. Getting together with other women to share your self-care journeys can be nurturing and fun. In *"Circles of Sharing,"* you will find guidelines for creating a women's sharing group, as well as many activities just for groups. Throughout the individual activity chapters, you will notice this symbol, ✿, that indicates the activity would work well with groups.

As a special offering, we end the book with "Women's Stories." These are the voices you will hear in sidebars throughout the book as they accompany you on your journey, and their stories are gathered together at the end of the book as a special bonus. You can read more about their journeys through life, their challenges and joys, how they take care of themselves, advice for others, and what they celebrate about being women. The women we interviewed come from many different backgrounds, are different ages, and

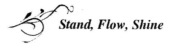

live in a variety of geographic locations. They represent, in a small sample, the vast diversity of women.

Using the Book

Find what appeals to you in these chapters. If your life is busy, it may be best to go to a specific section to find an activity that will fit your needs. We encourage you to bring your own experience to these pages and to approach the book in your own way.

~ "Stand Tall Like the Tree" can point the way to creating some emotional changes, as well as changes in thinking and attitude. You may recognize and celebrate what personal self-empowerment means for you.

~ You will find in "Flow Like the River" gentle movements for the body and creative activities for self expression.

~ You may turn to "Shine Like the Sun" and try a relaxation process or meditation.

~ You can mix up the order and try out the activities and processes in any way that is comfortable for you.

Our primary piece of advice for you is to keep on doing the processes, over and over. Build your emotional muscle, strengthen your connection with your inner wisdom, and take good care of your physical body.

What are you facing in your life right now? Are you feeling stressed? Wondering how to find time for you? Needing a boost to your confidence? Feeling stuck and wanting to move forward? We have created a few self-care plans for specific concerns. Perhaps one of these plans fits you now.

Self-Care Plans

Feeling Stressed?

You have so much going on in your life that pulls you in so many directions. Some of the stressors you are prepared for; others

come from unpredicted events or changes in your life. Whatever the sources of your stress, you are feeling the need for relaxation and ease in your life.

Flow Like the River:
> Body in Motion
> Flowing with Music

Shine Like the Sun:
> Guided Relaxations
> Relaxing Musical Journeys
> Nurturing Yourself
> Five New Comfort Activities
> Treating Yourself with Kindness
> Mindfulness Meditations

Finding Time for You?

You really don't feel you have any time to give to yourself. You have so many other priorities. So here are suggestions for some activities that are easy and don't take long. Move along at your own pace.

Read Marilyn's and Judith's lists in "Why Is Self-Care Important?" and adopt anything from those lists that is an easy fit into your day.

Stand Tall Like the Tree:
> Daily Messages to Yourself
> Self-Care Action Plan

Flow Like the River:
> Breath of Joy
> Free-Form Drawing and Poetry

Shine Like the Sun:
> Walking Meditation
> Journal Reflections
> Self-Care Writing
> Morning/Nighttime Writing
> Feelings Check-In

Building Your Confidence?

You want to feel more sure of yourself. You need to build an inner core of strength and self-empowerment. Regularly repeating any of these processes and activities can be strengthening.

Stand Tall Like the Tree:
> ALL processes could be helpful

Flow Like the River:
> Easy Flow
>
> Self-Empowerment Postures

Shine Like the Sun:
> Sitting and Walking Meditations

Feeling Stuck and Wanting to Move Forward?

You want to feel more engaged with your life. It is difficult to take those first steps towards getting unstuck. Make an easy commitment to do one process today and see where that goes for you. Start with something that does not require discipline but is just fun.

Stand Tall Like the Tree:
> Letting Go
>
> Moving Forward
>
> Positive Self-Talk
>
> Self-Care Action Plan

Flow Like the River:
> Free-Form Drawing and Poetry
>
> Relaxation and Visualization Script 1 or 2
>
> Easy Flow

Remembering the Self-Care Processes

One of the biggest challenges of taking good care of yourself is being able to remember to use the processes that you have learned. This is a challenge every day and, especially, in a situation when you are particularly stressed. Until self-care becomes part of your daily routine, here are some easy ways to help you remember:

~ Place reminder notes throughout your home, and even at work, if you can. (Put notes next to your bed and on something you use every day, such as your toothbrush holder or mirror.)

~ Use a particular bracelet on your wrist as a visual reminder.

~ Use your cell phone timer or alarm clock as a sound reminder.

Use these tips often to establish new positive habits. They can become a part of your daily care, like brushing your teeth. All of this takes take very little time. The more you make self-care routines a daily habit, the more they will be remembered in the midst of a hard time.

Beginning Your Self-Care Journey

Create your sanctuary.

My little room in my house is a source of support. I have a place in my house where I can go. It is a sanctuary, definitely. –Susan

Creating a sanctuary, no matter how small, can be the perfect start for your self-care journey. It can be your own special room or part of a room. In this space, you create a safe, nurturing, and fulfilling place. Colors and textures may define this environment. To inspire your creativity and soothe your soul, you might have pillows, books, music, art materials, journals, pictures, candles, incense, and favorite things from the natural world. This is your safe, sacred haven: your sanctuary.

Keep a journal.

You might enjoy creating a journal of your experiences with the activities in this book that you could title "My Self-Care Journey." The journal doesn't have to be fancy. You might take a notebook and cover it with pictures or artwork. Or you might open a new file on your computer, if this is a good way for you to journal.

6

Whatever you use, your experience will deepen if you write about a process while you are doing it or soon afterward. You can use your journal also as a place to record ideas, thoughts, insights, and feelings as you go along, as well as for artwork. Reviewing your journal now and then will serve as a good reminder of the journey you are taking.

> While following the processes in the book, you may want to have something you can use to keep the pages open and flat. For instance, you could use two pretty stones, two large clips, or a cookbook holder.

Why Is Self-Care So Important?

When you take good care of yourself, you become healthier physically, mentally, and emotionally. You have more energy for your own life when you make yourself a priority. Your physical and emotional wellness flourishes when you treat your body with care and compassion. You are replenished and restored when you give yourself time and attention. You find inner strength as you clear emotional blocks and thought patterns that get in your way. And, when you experience relaxation, meditation, and creative play, you reduce stress and increase peacefulness and pleasure.

In this book, we emphasize taking care of you first. It is time to take care of you with kindness, sensitivity, and resourcefulness. Then, from this reserve of energy and well-being, this place of self-caring and compassion, you can deepen your caring and compassion for others and the world around you.

Marilyn:

Making a place for me in my life was an ongoing challenge. Sometimes I would be absolutely on track with finding me in my life, and other times, me was at the bottom of a stack of messy papers on my desk. Now, after living through several losses, including the most unexpected—the death of my husband of thirty-five years—I was forced to stop and take stock of how I was living my life.

These changes have opened my heart, forced me to accept what would have seemed unacceptable, and led me to practice self-care as

the best route to surviving with a hope for the future. I have come to believe that there is a way through, even in the most difficult of times. This way through is rooted within me, where loving care, respect, and compassion for me and others reside in timeless silence. I reach this inner place when I engage in self-care activities. They are lifelines in times of crisis. I know this from firsthand experience.

When I am taking care of myself, I feel grounded and happy. I walk, exercise, and practice yoga. I read novels. I enjoy making my home beautiful. I give attention to the people I love, especially my family and my community of caring friends. I take personal reflecting time to create mandalas and collages, meditate, and listen to music. I feel and express my grief and my joy. I love myself for letting me be in my life. I am learning to balance my own needs with the urge to take care of others. I feel peaceful and centered from time to time.

What Does Self-Care Mean?

The key to taking good care of you is nurturing yourself. Nurturing means giving love, care, compassion, appreciation, support, honesty, and openness. It means giving directly and freely to you. It also means receiving care and support from others.

✐ I've reached a stage in life where I'm comfortable in my skin. I'm more confident than I was as a younger person. I am who I am, and that's how it's going to be. I'm not going to change into a new person at this age. But warts and all, this is who I am. I accept myself. –Gloria ✐

Learn to nurture yourself by first reflecting on what you know about yourself. What are your own particular needs? How do you listen to yourself? Do you accept yourself with love and compassion?

Accepting, smiling, even laughing at yourself at times are essential to nurturing yourself. It is the ability to stand back and say, "Yes, this is me, all of me. I can do some things, and I can't do others. I am who I am." To say, "This is good about me; that is great!" or "Whoops, here I am, doing that one again!" You learn to accept the many parts of yourself that make you who you are.

When you also remind yourself of your strengths and all that you can do, you give yourself a boost to move ahead on your self-care journey. You will see that you can develop and retain a sense of perspective, understanding, and humor about yourself.

Discover ways to make yourself feel better even when you are feeling upset or stressed. Find what works for you. Learn simple ways to reduce stress and anxiety. You might begin by asking yourself these questions:

~ How can I make myself feel better here?
~ What can I do for myself that will be good for me?
~ Is this enhancing my well-being?
~ How can I keep myself centered?

Make yourself a priority by doing something nice that you know you enjoy. Put time aside that you will spend just with yourself— your special time. This is a way of feeding back into you some of the energy and attention that you are always putting out—with work, relationships, children, house, and simply getting from one day to the next.

The first and most important way I nurture and take care of myself is taking on board the fact that I should take care of myself and deserve to take care of myself. It starts there, just from a mindset of "that's what you need to do," especially if you are a parent and you are used to taking care of your kids. You get out of the habit of thinking about what your needs are. It's coming back and saying, "Okay, yes, you do need to nourish yourself and take care of yourself." –Toby

Take a long, warm bath; give yourself a gift; take a quiet walk; spend some time in silence; listen to music—letting it fill you; give yourself a massage—recognize, accept, and, yes, enjoy this body of yours. These activities do not have to take a long time.

> **The point is that you are communicating these messages to yourself:**
> "I am important and special."
> "I need and deserve special care."
> "I will do this for myself."

When replenishing your own energy becomes routine, you no longer have to depend on others to be the source for these good feelings. Any additional nurturing from others becomes further enhancement and enjoyment of what you are already giving and doing for yourself.

Judith:

I am sitting in my little room, my sanctuary. I look around, and I see shells, stones, candles, crayons, music CDs, books, photos, pottery, beautiful wood surfaces, and soft cushions.

I feel nurtured, nourished, renewed, and calmed. I sit in the midst of this space that sustains me and brings me back to myself. I come here regularly. I close the door, unplug the phone, and play beautiful, inspiring music. I come here to regain myself, to touch the core of myself, and to remember my deep caring for others, the natural world, and me. In this space, I am safe and soft.

Within this safety and softness, I sometimes want to reconnect with some of my deepest feelings, opening my heart to whatever pours through and out. I let my feelings flow, allowing grief, anger, sadness, or loss to open portions of my heart. Reconnecting with feelings of joy and gratitude furthers my connection with myself and my well-being. I know that when I am open and accepting of whatever feeling I experience, I am taking good care of myself.

I have my journals next to me. I listen to some lovely, gentle music. I write my feelings and thoughts and read out loud what I have written. I read books that inspire my creativity and remind me of the beauty of life.

What I write and read has so much meaning and healing for me. This space is a womb for me, a place to birth myself. This is the place where I can finally create for myself an internal life of calm and peace, safety and well-being. Here I am surrounded by favorite sounds, sights, and textures, bathing myself with warm soothing light inside and out. I have come here to find and to hold and to cherish myself 'til never do I part.

Stand, Flow, Shine

**We asked many women, "What do you do to feel nurtured?"
Here are some of their responses:**

> I remember to do what calms me.
>
> I take care of myself through meditation and a daily workout.
>
> I remember what makes me feel good: rest, taking classes, playing music.
>
> I have found a spiritual community that I enjoy and find meaningful.
>
> I read good books, drink tea, and remember to breathe.
>
> My friends are important, so I go out with them.
>
> I play hooky and feel good about it. I know that things will still be there to be done when I get back.
>
> I cook good meals with good ingredients. I eat with no distractions.

It is also important to know how others can participate in your self-care. Consider setting up an agreement with certain people, acknowledging your need to be nurtured at times. There may be people in your life who give you support regularly or just at the time you seem to need it most. There may be some people with whom you have an understanding: you give to them, and they give to you.

Learn to clarify what you need. For example, you could ask:

~ I need to talk over some problems. Can you hear me out?

~ I need some support while I'm thinking about making some changes in my life.

~ I need to cry some—on the phone or with you. Can you come over, or can I go over there?

~ Would you give me a hug?

These questions or statements can be quite difficult to state out loud. Perhaps you have too much pride, or a fear that you will never get it anyway, so why ask? Well, all people need human connection and support just as much in their adulthood as when they were children.

13

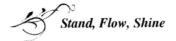

❧ I knew a woman who said, "I limit myself to four things." She said to me, "Are you married? That's one. Do you have children? That's two. Do you run this house?" Holy smokes, that's already three! I just took those things for granted. As a result, I was always running behind. I've really appreciated that advice. There is a certain limit. –Susan ❧

Learning to take good care of you also means learning to set limitations and boundaries on your time and energy when caring for others. Recognize what you can and cannot do. Setting limits is not always easy. It can be hard to say no. You might worry that you are being insensitive or selfish or that others will stop caring about you. Spend some time clarifying mutual limitations, and the relationships can withstand the limits and even grow stronger.

Why Is It So Hard to Take Care of Yourself?

We have thought about, talked about, and researched the question: why do women not take better care of themselves? Here are some reasons we have found that may begin to explain why a woman can lose the connection with herself, starting from childhood.

❧ When I was a little girl, I wore all kinds of frilly things, and I was really into it. It was only when I saw how my mother was treated, that mothering and nurturing were just not seen as important, that I said, "Okay, I'm not going to be that." –Leah ❧

The girl-child may live in a world where the values of caring and connection are seen as inferior to assertiveness and independence. She learns in a subtle (or not so subtle) way that caring and connection, while approved of and appreciated, may not be recognized as valuable.

Along with this, her intuitive ability—that inner knowing—may be downplayed in deference to others' explanations of how things are in the world. When her inner sense and values are not met by the outer world, she may abandon them in order to fit in more comfortably with the status quo. She may come to doubt her own worth and put others' opinions and values before her own.

Caring for others may come naturally to you, and you may find that you are appreciated for all that you do. So you learn to set aside your needs and to always extend your empathy to others. You may feel that in caring for others you are caring for yourself. You lose your connection to yourself when you repeatedly put others' concerns above your own. Indeed, you may feel that it's selfish and self-indulgent to consider your own needs. Or, you may just feel uncomfortable with the notion of focusing so much attention on yourself.

Your challenge is to become comfortable with recognizing, stating, and meeting your needs. A new sense of yourself emerges as you no longer feel guilty about making a commitment to your self-care. Loving yourself, having compassion for yourself, and giving care to yourself enliven you and bring balance into your life. You are beginning to make yourself a priority in your own life.

Think about Your Own Journey

You are the best person to take care of you. Once you embark on this journey, and find how easy self-care is and how good it feels, you will want to make this commitment to your self-care. No one will ever take better care of you than you—because you are the one who really knows what you need and how to get it.

◢

Judith:
What I have learned to do to take care of myself

Have a space of my own, my sanctuary.

Feel my love for my family, friends, and all others.

Catch myself about to be critical and turn this around to something positive.

Get moving—walking, yoga, tai chi.

Meditate.

Keep a journal.

End each day by writing five experiences and people for which I am grateful.

Call a friend for support.

Listen to music, close my eyes, and let it fill my body.

Read inspiring books that can make my life better.

Set aside time regularly for creative play.

Write out all that gives me hope.

Marilyn:

What I have learned to do to take care of myself

Accept what each day brings.

Make peace with my inner child's needs by recognizing and feeling my feelings.

Say "no" to new responsibilities unless they really fit well into my life.

Pay attention to the cues from my body to eat, not eat, exercise, rest, etc.

Don't live in regret for what might have been.

Practice mindfulness meditation and yoga.

Find wonder and serendipity in each day.

Laugh and cry.

Call a friend.

Have patience.

Drive carefully.

Be kind and generous.

Be grateful.

Forgive.

Dance.

Sing.

Stand Tall Like the Tree

A tree stands in the forest, straight and graceful. She has seen and experienced a lot in her long life. Her strong core and solid roots are what have given her longevity. While strong and steady, she can bend and ease in the wind. Seasons change; she changes and yet stays balanced. You, too, can stay focused and in a state of balance even when your life is being blown around by strong forces over which you have little control. Self-care practices help to send your roots deep and strengthen your core beliefs in yourself.

In this chapter, we address your attitudes toward yourself. Unconscious behaviors, thought patterns, and old beliefs about yourself can limit your potential and make you feel unsure of yourself. When you give yourself positive messages and think about yourself with love and compassion, your old negative patterns will melt away.

It's a challenge to really go out there and face fear as a woman and to stand tall and to say, "I can do it; I can do it!" And have that determination within yourself. You can overcome a lot of stuff. You can overcome mountains! —Joyce

Like the tree, you can sway with the forces of change while staying rooted. By being flexible and strong, you help your sense of self-empowerment grow. You will grow to appreciate your own worth. You stand tall. This is tree. This is you.

In this chapter:

Changing Attitudes and Behaviors

Letting Go
Moving Forward
Mental Rehearsal to Prepare for Challenges
A Change of Attitude
Redirecting Your Thoughts
Gathering "Wows!"
Positive Self-Talk

Daily Messages to Yourself

Daily Letting Go
Setting a Daily Intention
Affirming Yourself
Anchoring a Positive Message

Developing Inner Strength

Your Self-Empowerment Story
Positive Possibilities
Giving Voice and Being Heard
Obstacle Course
Your Self-Care Action Plan

Changing Attitudes and Behaviors

Every day is a new opportunity to be in charge of how you feel and what you do. Rather than dwelling on the experiences of the past or worries about the future, you can shape how you want to be today. Although you cannot control everything that happens to and around you, you can have more control over how you want to feel and how you want to take yourself through these experiences. Make a change in your attitude, and this will positively affect your behavior.

Letting Go ✿

Are you ready to move toward being how and who you want to be? Get ready to *let go* of some old stuff! What do you need to let go in order to really feel good? Think of a feeling or a behavior that gets in the way of your well-being.

We like to do this process outside, but it can be done anywhere.

Outdoors, in nature, and preferably near a stream: Find a twig, leaf, or stone, and let it become the symbol for the feeling or behavior you want to release.

Take a moment to think about how this feeling or behavior might have taken care of you at some time. You now have new ways to take care of yourself. Thank that feeling or behavior for taking care of you in the past. Now take a deep breath, and let it go, saying what you are letting go. You can toss the object into a flowing stream, off the side of a hill, or bury it. Let yourself truly feel the letting go.

For example, a woman who grew up in a chaotic household learned to deny her own feelings and be quiet in order to feel safe. As she tosses a leaf into a stream, she says, "I no longer have to deny my feelings!"

Indoor variation: If you are indoors, take a paper and pen, and write down what the feeling or behavior is that you want to let go. Say out loud what it is you are letting go, and tear the paper

into small pieces. You could throw away the bits of paper, burn them in a fireplace, or immerse them in water, watching the words disappear.

Indoors or outside, take a deep breath, relax, and let go. Affirm for yourself that you have let go of an old pattern in your life and that you are moving forward. Believe in yourself and your ability to become who you want to be.

Moving Forward ✿

After the Letting Go process, take a few slow, calming breaths. Think of how you want to move forward with a new feeling or behavior. Word it in the present as if it is already true: "I am free to express myself," "I take good care of myself," "I am peaceful and calm." Anchor this new, positive message by taking a deep breath in and stating the message inside again as you breathe out. You may want to hold a little stone or some other meaningful object as you anchor your new message. This object can be a reminder for you in the future. Keep it in a pocket or a noticeable place.

Mental Rehearsal to Prepare for Challenges

Are you anticipating a difficult conversation with someone, a job interview, an employment evaluation, a new dating opportunity, or some other challenging situation? The mental rehearsal can help you increase your self-confidence as you approach any situation that causes you stress or anxiety.

You start your mental rehearsal by remembering a time when you felt really confident and letting the memory bring you that positive feeling. Anchor a message of confidence (such as "I can do this!" or "I am confident and ready!") by taking a slow, deep breath in, and as you slowly, deeply exhale, hear that message, and feel it deep inside. Repeat two more times.

Think about an upcoming situation that might be difficult or challenging. Anchor your message of confidence again. In your

imagination, take yourself through this situation, step by step. Any time you come to a difficult place or an obstacle, anchor your message with your deep breathing. Notice how you take yourself through that hard part. Continue on with all the details you can anticipate, anchoring your message, and watching how you take yourself through each difficult part until you come to the end. Again, anchor your message three times.

Take out your journal, and write your anchored message, your positive feelings, and any reflections you have about handling this anticipated situation and others that may arise.

Before you go into any challenging situations, remember to anchor your message and visualize your success! You now have a positive resource to prepare you for difficult, stressful situations: the mental rehearsal.

> ✍ *I really value the ability to be strong. One of my fantasies and goals when I was young was to be able to stand in a room and say "No" and to be strong in my position when everyone else had a different position. I could visualize that, and it was very powerful. I value that "I can" attitude.*
> *–Karen* ✍

A Change of Attitude

If you find yourself frequently complaining and judging others, this negativity is often a call for change. Frequent criticism and negativity can wear down a relationship, whether it is at work, with a friend, or in the family. Our negative attitudes may come from insecurity and anxiety. You may feel that the details of your life are out of your control, and you attempt to manage this feeling by focusing on negative aspects of others. You might think, "If only I could get so-and-so to change this one habit or behavior, then I would feel back in control and okay."

Unfortunately, thinking negative thoughts and wishing that someone else might change are not likely to get you what you hoped for. Dealing with your own underlying anxieties and insecurities (with professional help, if necessary) will help change this behavior, and you will feel better.

It's really important for you to be able to catch yourself, to understand, and to remind yourself why you're about to say something critical. Then you can take a deep breath and, instead, say something positive to the person. Saying something positive has many benefits:

~ It reminds you that there really are positive aspects to this person.

~ It gives you something pleasant to say and takes care of the impetus to say something negative.

~ It makes you feel better, emotionally and physically.

There is a physiological difference between tightening up for an unpleasant comment and softening for a pleasant one. The body relaxes, and the emotions ease. By behaving this way, you are taking better care of yourself and your relationships.

Redirecting Your Thoughts

Do you obsess or worry? Going over thoughts again and again, particularly negative ones, can be depleting. When you keep repeating a worry or concern (obsessing), you can create pathways of thought that keep you stuck. You become susceptible to these habits of thinking.

You can learn to redirect your thoughts by being mindful of this habit and consciously changing it. Without judging yourself, pay attention to your thoughts. When you catch yourself obsessing, say "Obsessing." Then add "I can soothe myself. I'm all right." Take a slow, deep breath because this helps to calm and focus your mind away from the negative thoughts. Developing a new thought pathway could even become a light-hearted practice if you say "Gotcha, obsession!" Follow this playful response with a soothing deep breath and a big smile. This will definitely lighten up these thought patterns.

Gathering "Wows!"

Do you take yourself from one activity to another without stopping to take in and appreciate the positives that are present? In this easy daily practice, take note of something that makes you feel and say, "Wow!" It could be something as simple as looking at the sky or a beautiful tree. It might be feeling gratitude towards a friend or a loved one. Notice the change in how you feel about yourself and your day as you gather "wows" throughout the day. See if you can make this a lovely, daily habit. You might even record them in your journal at the end of each day.

Positive Self-Talk

Do you have a habit of talking down to yourself? Do you ever catch yourself saying something like, "That was dumb!" or "I never get it right"? Fill in your own well-used put-downs. As you strengthen your commitment to self-care, being overly hard on yourself is *off limits*. Take care of yourself by taking control of the way you talk to yourself. Learn to appreciate

When I hear those old messages creeping up, I talk to myself and say "No! No! You can give yourself a new message." That's been very helpful. I feel empowered when I do that. –Karen

yourself. Have compassion for yourself. Trust yourself. Trust does not come easily where there is too much criticism.

To better care for yourself and to truly grow in self-love, create new habits of self-talk. When the criticism begins, say "Good-bye" or "Off limits!" Accept that you make mistakes and that you are doing the best you can. Then take a few good, quality breaths, and affirm for yourself that you are taking care of yourself in new, positive ways.

> **Replace the negative statements with a positive message or affirmation, such as:**
> "I can make myself okay with the decisions I make."
> "Sometimes I may make a mistake—I am only human."
> "I am a good person."
> "I am who I am."

25

Daily Messages to Yourself

There are many ways that you can calm and center yourself every day. You may find it helpful to practice one or more of these processes daily to keep yourself emotionally steady. In addition, they can be used in times of stress, confusion, or negativity. Each of the following processes is somewhat different from the others, but they all have the same goal: *care for you.*

Daily Letting Go

Begin with a few deep breaths. Identify any feelings or behaviors that might get in the way of your being really present and centered. After recognizing what these might be (such as worrying, criticizing yourself, or holding onto resentments and anger), breathe out and let each one go. Say "I am releasing ..." Experience the sensation of releasing these feelings or behaviors. You will feel much lighter. Now set an intention for the day.

Setting a Daily Intention

Setting a daily intention is an empowering way to feel more in control, and it can help carry you through your day. The intention can be a specific, concrete goal (to eat a healthy lunch, return phone calls or emails, or get some exercise). An intention can also reflect a feeling or general way of being. For example, one morning you set the intention "I can give myself calm and ease whenever I need it." When you find yourself in a stressful or difficult situation, remember your intention. Remind yourself: "Wait! I can give myself calm and ease whenever I need it, and I need it now!" Then take three slow, deep breaths. Repeat your intention, and let calm and ease flow all through your body, mind, and spirit.

> **Here are some examples of daily intentions:**
> "I will take really good care of myself today."
> "I will be relaxed and mindful throughout my day."
> "Today I will work on being more organized."

Deepen your intention by anchoring it with three slow, deep breaths. Each time you exhale, hear and feel the intention deep inside. This is a wonderful way to start your day.

Affirming Yourself

An affirmation is a variation of the daily intention. Stating and holding a positive affirmation will empower you and help you strengthen your self-esteem. Let affirmations become part of your daily routine.

> **State the affirmation as if it were already happening,** for instance:
> "I am a calm, serene woman."
> "I am strong and self-reliant."
> "I make decisions, and I am okay with them."
> "I am taking good care of myself."
> "I am taking good care of my body."

Post your intentions and affirmations in handy places (put stick-it notes on the refrigerator, bathroom mirror, and computer, or text yourself). Any way that you remember to affirm yourself will work. The most important part of this daily activity is that you are creating a new set of positive messages for your well-being. You are learning to live with intention, purpose, and awareness.

Anchoring a Positive Message

✐ I have a little stone that I take with me. When I start feeling sorry for myself, I say, "Okay, Joyce, how are you going to do it? It is just you, and you have so many things going on, and you want to take care of everybody." I hold that stone, and that is my strength. I am saying to the stone as I squeeze it, "You are going to take my burdens; you are going to let me feel better." It's like the little stone says, "Okay, are you going to choke me to death? I heard you!" And that really keeps me smiling. Whatever we get strength from, we can use as a tool to get over our difficult times.
—Joyce ✐

Anchoring a positive daily message is similar to setting a daily intention and affirmation. You can think of it as creating an anchor, as though you are placing it within yourself to come back to whenever you need positive reinforcement. First thing in the morning, throughout the day, and before you go to sleep, repeat your anchored message to yourself. Repeating a positive, simple message helps change the earlier messages you may have received in your life. As a child, you may have heard negative or hurtful messages.

After a while, you could become "hardwired" with these messages, acting out and becoming the messages you heard. The more you give yourself new, positive messages, the more you may actually begin to believe them. You can act from these new messages instead of from the old ones.

Tell yourself that you can be the way you want to be; you have the power within you. Enjoy the good feelings of strength, ability, confidence, and competence. Now, holding onto these feelings, listen inside yourself for a message—a phrase or a sentence—that will remind you of this inner strength and power. For example, the message might be "I can do this. I have what it takes." Anchor the message three times.

> **Some other positive messages might be:**
> "I can handle what comes my way."
> "I am alright just as I am."
> "I am a good person."
> "I am a capable woman."

Anchor a new, positive message for yourself right now! Give yourself a message you need to hear today.

Developing Inner Strength

A woman who is courageous and strong has poise and self-confidence and is not afraid to speak up. She is at ease with herself in any situation. She has an inner strength, a felt sense that she can act with confidence in the world. This inner strength is what we call *self-empowerment.*

To be empowered does not mean having power over someone or something, but, instead, it is a feeling of inner strength, confidence, and capability. With this feeling, we can take ourselves through difficult situations with self-assurance. Feeling and being empowered come with practice, experience, and belief in you. The strong, tall tree with its inner core strength is an apt image for self-empowerment.

> **How do women feel empowered? Here are some answers from women in our workshops:**
>
> I am free to make decisions about my life and to know myself. I don't have to prove myself.
>
> It is empowering to overcome the scary times and to trust myself. I have done it before, so I can do it again.
>
> I take care to recharge: being at home, being outdoors, connecting to something bigger than myself.
>
> I continue to seek new experiences, set new goals, and meet new challenges.
>
> I reflect back on my accomplishments.
>
> It is empowering to accept myself and to use the strengths I have been given.
>
> I see my grandmother in my children. I think back, and I think forward. I'm not the only one facing the challenges I face. This has been done before.

The processes described here can help you find inner confidence and strength—your empowered self. The first process shines a light on your past, highlighting a time when something you did made a positive difference.

Your Self-Empowerment Story ✿

Take a few moments to relax and make yourself comfortable. Have your journal nearby. You can quiet your body and mind quickly by simply focusing on your breathing. Breathe in; breathe out. Do this for a few moments until you feel your body relaxing and your mind quieting. Now begin to think about a time when something you did or said made a positive difference. The event may or may not have involved someone else. It may have been something small, large, or anything in-between. Remember the event as fully as you can, bringing details of the memory into your mind. The following questions will spark your memories of the event:

Where were you?

Who was there?

What did you do or say?

How did it make a difference?

How did you feel?

How do you feel about the event now?

This is your *self-empowerment story*!

In your journal, write down the highlights of the story, being sure to write about how what you did made a positive difference. Read it over to yourself, and take in the fact that you have made a positive difference in the world. You might draw a picture or symbol of that event. You can do this exercise many times, finding affirmation of your own strength and courage. You may find that speaking the story out loud is affirming and empowering.

Self-Empowerment Stories

Lena's Story

I remember there was a time when I was a child growing up in Jamaica that my father had the flu, and he couldn't go to work. Everybody in that house had the flu. They had a lot of goats, miles away from the house. I had to go there and take care of all of them. I was scared, but I had to go, or they would die. I was the only person in the house who wasn't sick. It was about four miles in the woods I had to go and take care of those goats: take them from one location to the other and give them fresh food. When I was going home, I felt good in myself that I was able to do that. When I got home, my father was so happy. He said, "My daughter, I thank you so much. You are so brave!" After I went home, I cooked for twelve people. That's what I did.

Aisha's Story

I was going through engineering school. I was one of three women in the program and the only one in excelled math class. And when we had group projects, the guys would say "Oh, you can be the secretary." Why do I need to be the secretary? In my other job when I was doing layout engineering work, they tried to make me clean the office. I told them, "Ya'll hired me to do layout work. Why am I cleaning your office? If you feel that I need to do this, then everybody needs to take a day out of the week and do this." Then they changed the whole thing up and said, "Oh, okay. Never mind." You know, just proving them wrong, doggone it! I really enjoyed that.

Marge's Story

I guess the thing that gave me the biggest kick about being a woman was that I was in a profession where there were so

very few women. It made me kind of special and also kind of on the outside.

I graduated from medical school in 1935, so I started pretty early, and there weren't many other women until about the next year or two, and then little by little women have been taking over medicine, or at least half of it!

Positive Possibilities

You are always in a process of becoming. Each day brings some new learning and some small change. Your self-concept may have some old, leftover messages of inadequacy. How do you want to be living your life? And most of all, what do you want to believe about yourself? This process encourages you to imagine who you could become.

Set aside time for yourself. Make yourself comfortable. Relax with the help of some slow, deep breaths. Now anchor a message of encouragement (such as "You can do this" or "I believe in you") by taking a slow, deep breath in, and as you slowly, deeply exhale, hear that message, and feel it deep inside. Repeat two more times.

Who do you want to become? Picture yourself. How would you dress? How would you move? How would you interact with people? What would you do and say if you were just the way you want to be? Let an image come to mind that expresses the answers to these questions and that captures this sense of becoming. Feel this in your body and emotions. Take a slow, deep breath, and anchor your message again.

As the Olympic athlete imagines her perfect athleticism, you imagine that you are now who you want to be. Once again, take it in, letting yourself feel the positive possibilities. Picture yourself in many situations: easy ones and difficult ones. See yourself handling them. Feel yourself being just how you want to be. Take a few more, slow, deep breaths. Anchor your message again.

You can deepen this new definition of yourself by writing a few phrases, a story, or poem; drawing a picture; dancing; singing; or striking a pose of the new you.

Notice the change in how you treat yourself and how you interact with others. Repeat this activity whenever you feel the need to make a leap toward your ideal self.

Giving Voice and Being Heard ✿

It is so important for women to be heard, listened to, acknowledged, and respected. Early family experiences, educational systems, personal shyness, or lack of confidence can keep you from giving voice to your feelings, thoughts, opinions, and wishes. What if you did speak up? What if you did dare to be heard? Try giving voice to what's on your mind and in your heart. It is your right to speak and, yes, to assert yourself. You may want to begin with safe situations where you feel you will be heard and appreciated. Then, from time to time, try speaking out in more challenging situations, using the safety net of your own budding self-confidence. Take opportunities to be heard throughout your day. Speak what is on your mind or in your heart.

As a child I felt so unsure of myself and so unsettled as to what my place in the universe was. I didn't know what was good for me. It was always what was good for other people or what others were telling me. I come back to this image of my own voice because it's what I see symbolically as being important to me—and to anyone: to be able to hear one's own voice and let that voice out.
—Marian

Obstacle Course ✿

Often, when you set goals, there are obstacles that get in the way. Sometimes you are not aware what these obstacles are or even that they exist. The following process helps you identify, acknowledge, and deal with the obstacles that get in the way of your self-care journey. It can be done inside or outside with room to move around. If done with others, do not talk throughout the process.

33

~ *Begin by quieting yourself with three slow, deep breaths. Now think of a goal that would make your life better.* Such a goal could be a change in your behavior, feelings, attitude, taking on some new activity, or making a change in a relationship, etc.

~ *Identify three obstacles* that could get in the way of meeting it. You might, for example, feel resistance, fear, or negative self-talk get in the way of meeting that goal. Your obstacles also might be very specific, such as lack of money or time. Identify each obstacle with a name or a phrase. State the goal and the obstacles to yourself. You could write them in your journal.

~ *Set your goal.* Begin at one end of the physical space you're in. Look to the other end of the space, and take a few minutes to visualize your personal goal at that other end.

~ *Create the obstacles.* Set up chairs, tables, or any other available objects to create three separate piles throughout the space being used. These piles represent your obstacles. Be creative, using as many props as possible.

~ *Connect with yourself.* Stand at one end of the space (the end opposite the "goal"). Before you start to deal with your obstacles, imagine a pile of sand on the floor or the ground in front of you. This stands for your connection with yourself. Gather and hold the imaginary sand in both hands, cupped together like a bowl. Should your hands come apart at any point, the sand slides away, and you have lost your connection with yourself. You do not want to lose any of yourself in this process. If you do, you have to go back and get another pile of sand and start all over.

~ *Encounter the obstacles.* Now, holding onto this imaginary sand, approach each obstacle (each pile), one at a time. Stop in front of each obstacle, and once again, identify just what this obstacle is in your life. Think about what you would have to do to deal with this obstacle in your real life as you

make your way through, over, or around the pile (or deal with it in any other way that works for you). Once you feel you have dealt with it, go on to the next one.

~ *Reach the goal.* When you have worked your way through each obstacle and you finally reach the other end of the space, you have arrived at your goal! Affirm for yourself that achieving this goal is well within your capability and that it is possible to get there without losing the connection to your deepest sense of yourself. At this point, release the imaginary grains of sand any way you want to. Honor yourself with respect and gratitude for staying connected with yourself during this process.

~ *Savor the moment.* Taking as much time as you need, be aware of how you feel having met your goal. Feel this accomplishment, and enjoy the feeling! Now write what you have learned in your journal.

Your Self-Care Action Plan

The *action plan* is a simple tool for maintaining your self-care practices. You will feel encouraged and motivated when you remember the strengths and resources you have. With this plan, you may recognize obstacles that get in the way of your moving forward. You will set actual timelines for self-care actions, giving you a feeling of self-empowerment. Keep the action plan handy, and refer to it in the future to see how you have accomplished your goals. You might also enjoy doing this activity with a good friend.

✎ If you take a step in any direction, things will come towards you. Once you have said, "I'm going to do this little thing," and you are willing, other things present themselves. Invitations start to come when you say yes to something. –Susan ✎

Use your journal to write the answers to the questions. As you make this commitment to take care of yourself, you may want to create a way to be accountable to yourself. Perhaps you could put a note on your mirror, your refrigerator, or in your cell phone that will remind you of this commitment to yourself.

Self-Care Action Plan*
- ~ Think of something that you could do to make your life better now. What would it be?
- ~ What strengths and resources do you have now that would help you do that?
- ~ What will you need to learn or acquire?
- ~ What obstacles might arise that could keep you from fulfilling this goal?
- ~ What might you be able to do to get past these obstacles?
- ~ What can you do in the next twenty-four hours—no matter how small the step—that will help you reach that goal?
- ~ What will you do in the next two weeks that will help you continue to make your life better?

Action Plan Variations

Think of something you could do to:
- ~ Enhance your creative flow
- ~ Feel more empowered
- ~ Nurture yourself
- ~ Bring inner peace into your life
- ~ Increase your well-being at work

As you continue on your journey from Tree, imagine the sound of leaves rustling to remind you of your new positive messages to yourself. The tree's deep roots keep you in touch with your personal strength. The branches sway, showing you that you can adapt to change caused by forces outside yourself. Remember and embody these images as you get ready for the challenges of each day.

---

*Thanks to Barbara Hazard and Kevin McVeigh, from the Interhelp Network, for creating the initial form of this exercise.

Flow Like the River

The river is always flowing, always changing. It creates its path with constant movement. When it is strong and full, it moves with power. When rains are few, it becomes a slow trickle. Your life energy is like the flow of a river. At times you feel you are really in the flow. Life is good. You feel connected, creative, and happy. Other times, you may feel depleted, bored, or uninspired, or that you are going against the flow, meeting with resistance, and having difficulty expressing yourself. There are times when the flow is almost too intense or tediously slow. Like the river, you can allow movement, spontaneity, and adaptation to change. Like the river, you can travel with a rushing expression of speed, enthusiasm, and emotion, or you can drift slowly over the pebbles of your thoughts.

In this chapter, we focus on enjoyable ways of moving your body with conscious flow and the expression of creative energies.

In the "Body in Motion" section, we give you instructions for simple movement processes. When you pay attention to stretching and strengthening your body, you will feel rejuvenated. You will also find several ways to increase the flow of your breath, an important step toward healthy living.

✒ I take care of myself by not giving up the creative aspect that is always burning in me. I paint for me, not for anybody else, and it is wonderful. It's kind of telling the story of my heart in different ways. –Danute ✒

In the "Creative Flow" and "Flowing with Music" sections, you will find suggestions for simple creative processes. These can help you clear your own river dams that keep you from enjoying the expression of your creativity. Let yourself flow with spontaneity and pleasure as you free your spirit through art, music, and writing. Allow your expressive abilities to come forth, and experience the joy of flowing freely. With these processes, you can find enjoyment, confidence, and insight.

Before starting any of these activities, you may want to take a slow, deep breath and anchor a message such as "I can relax and let my creativity flow."

Look for these icons in this chapter:

⌨ This icon tells you that you can find this process on our website: www.StandFlowShine.com. Movement processes are shown in video clips. Relaxations and meditations are recorded and can be listened to through your computer or downloaded to your MP3 player or mobile device.

✿ This icon indicates that this process can easily be adapted for group use.

You will be introduced to more group processes in the Circles of Sharing chapter.

In this chapter:

Body in Motion

Easy Flow
Energizing Flow
Flow of Deepening Connection

Creative Flow

Free-Form Drawing and Poetry
Drawing a Mandala
Nature Sculptures
Making Collages

Flowing with Music

Draw with Music
Journal with Music
Musical Improvisation

Body in Motion

Celebrate your body through exercise. Stretching, yoga, tai chi, walking, running, and swimming – all are wonderful ways to feel relaxed and rejuvenated. The more you move your body regularly in some way, the more mental and physical energy you will have, and the more you will increase your overall happiness. Even if your mobility is limited, it is still possible to find ways to move, such as exercise in a chair.

One thing that I really, really enjoy about life is dancing. If you have a good dance, it's like you forget about this world, and you are alone in this lovely place. You let yourself go and enjoy what life is. I dance even in my dreams. I always have dreams of dancing in the clouds, going over mountains and valleys and just swaying. Everything feels so free, as if you are the only one on this earth. It really calms my spirit. It gives me hope. –Joyce

Exercise can be quite simple and easy or, if you prefer, more rigorous. With regular exercise, you will feel a lessening of anxiety and depression, and you will be moving along in your self-care journey.

When your body is doing well you can move through life with greater ease. Get reacquainted with your body. Always begin slowly, pacing yourself. To prepare for any kind of movement, warm up your body with easy stretching.

Stretching is a primary way to keep the body in good working shape. It is also a way to calm your mind. A good routine in the morning can set you up for the day. At night, a few gentle stretches can calm you into sleep.

The following movement processes are gathered from many places. Some are adapted from hatha yoga, some from tai chi, and some we have created. We offer them here as a good way to start your day or as a break in a busy day.

Easy Flow 🖥 ✿

Here are simple instructions for stretching and feeling a flow in your body. You can choose particular ones that you like or do the whole series.

42

✍ For Calming and Centering

Three Good Quality Breaths: Breathe slowly and deeply in and out three times.

✍ To Ease Tight Places

Coming into the Present: Gently stretch as if you are pushing away any obstacles, thoughts, or feelings that are keeping you from coming into this present moment. Stretch your arms out in all directions until you feel you have created a space for yourself.

✍ To Limber Your Body

Tree Stretch: Folding over, bending your knees, and touching as close to your toes as you can, imagine that you can gather up energy from your roots (feet and legs); now gently unfolding, bring your hands up your trunk (upper legs, stomach, chest); stretching your arms out, let the energy go out your branches (arms), to your leaves and blossoms (hands and fingers gently moving).

✍ To Wake Up the Body

Tap the Body: With your fingertips, gently tap your head, then face, neck, shoulders, down one arm to your hand, back up that arm from underneath, to your chest, down the other arm and back up underneath that arm, back to your chest, your belly, upper legs, lower legs, ankles, feet, backs of your legs, your bottom, whatever you can tap on your back, to your neck again, and, finally, back to your head. "Hello Body!"

This can also be done with gentle massage to these areas as a way to calm your body during difficult times or before sleep. "Relax Body."

✍ To Feel More Present

Tiger's Eyes: Cross your hands in front of you, palms facing in. Look at the spaces between your thumbs and index fingers. Imagine that these spaces are your *tiger's eyes.* They stand for something you want or need to let go, a feeling or a behavior that is in

your way. Think of what this might be. Name it. See it in your tiger's eyes. Take a slow breath in. As you slowly breathe out, open your hands, and slowly lower them back down, letting go of what has been in your way. Feel the release in your body and emotions as you drop your hands. Do this again if you need to.

✐ To Focus

Cloud Hands: Reach your left hand, palm facing you, in front and to the right. Focus on your left hand, and imagine that your hand is like a cloud moving through the sky. Slowly make an arc with your left hand in front of your body. Keep your focus on that palm as you move your left hand in front and across to the left until it comes to a resting place on your left side. Now focus on your right hand, palm facing you, in front and to the left, and make another cloud, slowly making an arc in front of your body, moving your right hand in front and across to the right until it comes to a resting place along the right side of your body. Repeat this flow a few more times.

✐ For Balance and Grounding

Mountain Pose: Stand tall, spine straight and aligned, feet solidly planted on the floor (about hips' distance apart), arms relaxed at sides, neck and shoulders relaxed. Breathe slowly and deeply. Relax. Feel yourself to be a mountain with your head in the clouds, and your feet planted firmly on the ground.

✐ For Strength and Power Within

Self-Empowerment Pose: Standing in Mountain Pose, raise your arms above your head, hands facing each other or in fists, shoulders and neck relaxed. Feel your inner strength and power.

> Your *dantien* is your center, your balance point. It is under your belly button. Find your *dantien* by hooking your left thumb in your belly button, and then lowering your left hand on your belly, place your right hand over the left.

✐ For Increasing Energy

10,000 Things: Begin by placing your hands on your *dantien*. Follow the movement directions as you say the words in quotes out loud or to yourself.

Hands reaching up	"Gathering in the energy of 10,000 things"
Hands to heart	"into my heart."
Open hands out	"I am open and receptive."
Reaching up again	"Gathering in the energy of the sun, the moon, the stars, and the planets"
Bring hands to *dantien*	"into my *dantien*."
Reaching out wide	"Gathering in the energy of the winds, the woods, the waters, and the wildlife"
Bring hands to *dantien*	"into my *dantien*."
Hands moving down body from head to toes	"I bathe myself in all this energy."
Swaying, with arms flowing around body	"And let it flow."

Repeat process two more times.

✐ For Calm and Centering As You Complete the Series

Three Good-Quality Breaths: Take three slow, deep breaths in and out.

Energizing Flow 💻

When you feel present in your body, you feel empowered and energized. These next movements come from the hatha yoga tradition. This is a great way to strengthen not only your physical core but also your emotional and spiritual core.

Breath of Joy: This movement combines with breathing to bring an exhilarating and warming effect. The breath is accentuated

with a three-part inhalation, one-part exhalation pattern. When you use an energetic pace, you will be able to do this with one breath.

From a grounded stance, bend your knees slightly, and have your arms at your side. As you inhale, straighten your knees, and stretch your arms straight up, fingertips pointing to the sky. Inhale some more while thrusting your arms out to the sides at shoulder height. Inhale even more, moving your arms back up. Now exhaling, bring your arms down to your side, bending your knees and preparing to start over again.

You need to do only about three of these to feel the joy! This exercise can give you a great boost of energy when you need it.

Self-Empowerment Postures: From a grounded stance, move your feet so that they are wider apart than your shoulders' width. Bend your knees slightly. Bring your hands together, palms together. Next, separate your palms, keeping your elbows bent, until your arms are out to either side, palms still facing each other. Now, from the center of your body, your *dantien*, feel your strength and centeredness. Take a good, strong breath in. Breathe out three times, right from your belly! You may want to make a sound with each breath out and feel your power more.

Now straighten your legs; straighten your arms up and out to the side. You have now formed a five-pointed star (the five points are your head, hands, and feet). You are a star! Hold this position for several moments. Feel your own empowerment within yourself. Let your arms gently drop, take a deep breath, and let it go slowly.

These postures are simple, rejuvenating, and empowering to do. You could start your day with them. Or you might do them sometime during the day when you want to feel centered and empowered.

Flow of Deepening Connection ✿

Choose some music that you enjoy. Take a few slow, deep breaths. Let the sound and feel of the music fill you up. Begin to move

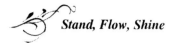
your body. Enjoy the feeling of the space around your body. Begin to feel how good it is to be connected with yourself. This is all you have to do—nothing else—just moving, just being with you.

Simply moving. Simply flowing. Not having to pay attention to structure or form or anyone else. It is a very pleasant way to connect with yourself and your body. Do it by yourself, with a partner, or with a group.

Creative Flow

Creativity is a major source for rejuvenation and well-being. Do you sometimes feel inhibited or embarrassed about your artistic expression? With these creative activities, you can push through old limitations and watch your creativity blossom. Set aside some time each week to let yourself stretch and grow creatively. We have included here a few projects that you might enjoy, along with instructions and lists of materials.

> 🖋 *I'm really clear that the balance of my creative work with clay has been tremendously sustaining in my other work and in the rest of my life. –Pat* 🖋

Free-Form Drawing and Poetry ✿

Loosen up your creative flow with this activity and have fun. Here you can create art and poetry—and no prior experience is required!

Materials:

- ~ Unlined paper or your journal
- ~ Pen or pencil
- ~ Coloring supplies such as crayons, markers, colored pencils

Music:

Listen to a short piece of music as you do this exercise. (You'll use only about 30 seconds.) Choose something that fits your intention for this exercise: calming, playful, energetic, changing your mood.

 *Stand, Flow, Shine*

Instructions:

Free-form Drawing

> ~ Have paper or your journal ready. Start the music and, holding a pen or pencil, close your eyes. Let your pen or pencil flow, making a continuous line over the paper, looping and winding around and around. Use the energy of the music to direct your flow on the paper. When you feel you have drawn a continuous looping line over most of your paper, turn off the music.

> ~ Open your eyes and look at your paper. Find shapes and color them in.

> ~ Look again at the shapes, and find a one-word title that fits the drawing you have made. Write this title at the top of the paper.

This is your drawing.

Free-Form Poetry

> ~ Turn your paper over (or go to the next page in your journal), and write the letters of the title vertically down the left-hand side of the sheet.

> ~ Write a line beginning with each letter. Do this quickly and spontaneously, writing whatever word, phrase or sentence comes to mind, starting with that letter. See the example below.

> ~ Now read each line.

This is your poem.

For example, your drawing has a peaceful feel to it; you name it "PEACE":

P	Perhaps peace is possible.
E	Each day we'll do what we can,
A	Always remembering to feel peaceful inside,
C	Caring and compassionate,
E	Each of us interconnected.

Drawing a Mandala ✿

Mandala means "magic circle" in the Sanskrit language. The circle is a symbol of wholeness and completion. It has no beginning and no end. Circles appear in organic forms in nature, art and architecture, our dreams, and the cycles of the seasons. When you draw a circle, you could think of it as a symbol of wholeness. Drawing within the circle can be a centering and meditative exercise. You may want to start a mandala journal, drawing one each day. Or you can draw a mandala on a day when you just feel you are being pulled in a lot of different directions and you need to center yourself. You can also draw a mandala to contain feelings that are difficult to express in words.

Materials:

~ Drawing paper, 11x14 is a good size although any size will do
~ A circular form, such as a plate, large enough to fill as much of the paper as possible
~ Various media such as oil pastels, chalks, colored pencils, markers

Instructions:

Take some time to center yourself. You might listen to some music, do some slow breathing, or meditate for a few minutes. Draw a circle using the circular form you have chosen. Look at the circle and decide where the center is. It might not be in the middle of the circle. Mark the center. With as little forethought as possible, choose colors and begin applying them to the circle. You can work quickly, or take all the time you want. Try to stay in a meditative, contemplative frame of mind throughout the time you are drawing.

When you have finished the mandala, look at it carefully, turning the paper around so you see your drawing from many different

angles and perspectives. Decide where the top of the mandala is, and put a small "t" in that place.

What would you title it? Let the title come quickly without much thought. Write it on the paper, on the side of the artwork, or on the back. Then, on either the front or back of the paper, write the date (and even the time of day, if you choose to).

In your journal, make a list of all the colors you used in your mandala. Think about what these colors mean to you. For example, "When I see bright orange, I think of fall leaves and pumpkins" or "When I see black, I think of a moonless night."

Make a list of all the forms you made. For example, there may be a form that looks like a seashell, or a hand, or a cup. Then make associations to those forms, trying to see what they may stand for: "This hand reminds me to reach out to others" or "This seashell reminds me of the importance of nature in my life."

As your associations become clear, a sense of meaning will begin to emerge from the mandala. Perhaps a theme is developing. Write all these ideas in your journal for further reflection. Put your mandala in a place where you can look at it from time to time.

Nature Sculptures ✿

With found objects, natural settings, and a little yarn or string, you can have a contemplative and enjoyable time in nature.

Materials:

~ String or yarn
~ Scissors or clippers
~ Colored paper
~ Natural items

Instructions:

- ~ Begin by setting a theme or intention for this creative session, such as "Whimsy," "Hidden Forms," or "Freeing Myself."
- ~ Gather materials such as small sticks and twigs, leaves, moss, flowers, dried seedpods, colorful paper, yarn or string. Try to use biodegradable items so that eventually your sculpture will return to the earth.
- ~ String, tie, prop, build, float (if you are working with water) the objects together, working at your sculpture until you feel it is done.
- ~ Consider all the elements. How will the wind blow this creation? When it rains, what will happen to the colors? Will the construction make it through the winter? Does it matter?
- ~ Stand back and enjoy it. You could name it and write about the process.

Variations:

Sculpture of Found Gifts: Find some things in nature that symbolize a gift you are giving to yourself. Create a sculpture. Enjoy the serendipity and fun of making a spontaneous work of art.

Journey Sculpture: Find things that represent where you are in your life. Put them together in a sculpture. You may want to add something that represents your past—where you came from—and your future—where you hope to go. You might add something to your sculpture that stands for your helpers along the way, your accomplishments, and any other aspects of your journey that arise in the creation process.

Making Collages ✿

Collage is an artistic composition made of scraps of paper, pictures from magazines, and other media such as foil, string, sticks, and

so on. All pieces are glued to the backing paper. Color and forms in the collage will emerge as you gather your materials together and begin to choose what you want to use. Some collages may be composed of torn paper fragments; others might include images carefully cut away from the original pictorial background. You may choose to use both torn and cut methods in one composition. Collages can be fun to make, with lots of energy generated in the process of choosing the paper, pictures, and other media and then finding just the right combinations of images and colors to put together. They can also provide a bridge between your deeper thoughts and feelings and your routine, everyday awareness.*

Intuitive Collage

Begin by setting the intention to be present and open to a particular theme or to whatever your intuition might bring to you.

Materials:

- ~ Stack of magazines
- ~ Scissors
- ~ Glue stick
- ~ Paper

Instructions:

Leaf through your stack of magazines and tear out anything that strikes you, in any way, positive or negative. After you've gathered an abundant pile of images, begin to sort through them. Which images want to play together for this collage? Don't overthink it, just follow your impressions. Set aside extra images. You may use them later.

Spread out the images, and look at them. Take your time. Play with them, shuffle them, and put them together in lots of different

---

*We thank Melanie Weidner, collage artist, for her instruction and her educational handouts, which we have used in our guidelines.

ways. Begin to look for a main character or two—images that seem central or right for now.

Carefully cut out your main images away from their background and put them together. Playfully add other images to your collage, looking for which images really want to be there—you may be surprised! Consider layering pictures to add more interest as a theme emerges.

At times you might feel stuck, unable to move forward with the collage. Take a little break and do something else, or go back to the magazines to find one or two more images that might be missing. Remember the pile that you set aside. There might be something there. Come back to the collage refreshed, and notice what new insight might pop up.

When you're ready to glue things down, look carefully to see which images you need to glue down first. Spread out a large piece of scrap paper, and place the cut-out images wrong side up on that paper. Swipe the glue stick from the center of the image out past the edge and onto the scrap paper. This ensures that you get glue all the way to the edges.

As you glue down the pictures, they may not look exactly as you imagined they would. That's okay. When you've finished gluing the collage, simply sit with the image you've created, and look for structures and patterns you hadn't seen before.

You can use the collage as a journal exercise. Give the collage a title, and write a brief description. Here are some questions you can ask yourself: What surprises you about it or about the process of making it? Which images appeal to you? What seems to be the main theme? If each main image had a voice, what would it say? Let the main images converse with each other. Write down the dialogue. If the collage were a dream you had, what might it be telling you?

Keep it in a safe place for the next several days so that you can look at it often.

Collage of Feelings

This activity requires no artistic skills and can put you in touch with your inner child and your creativity.

Sometimes you may experience an emotion that is hard to identify. Perhaps you aren't clear what you are feeling. Or you may feel stuck and just want the feeling to change. This collage can be a great way to let your feelings flow. Take a few moments to think about what feelings you may want to express or release.

Materials:

- ~ Several sheets of different colored construction paper
- ~ Glue stick
- ~ One large sheet of paper

Instructions:

- ~ Start with some deep, relaxing breaths, and invite those feelings to come forward. You might choose some music that supports your mood.
- ~ Choose the colors of construction paper you want and put them in front of you.
- ~ Close your eyes, and begin to tear up the paper randomly. After a while, open your eyes. Pay close attention to your feelings.
- ~ Place and glue your torn pieces on the large paper. Work until you feel the collage is finished.
- ~ Stand back from the collage. Take a look. Turn it around, viewing it from every angle. Decide which side you want to be the top.
- ~ Give it a title. Notice how you are feeling now.
- ~ Write in your journal about the feelings you had while making the collage. Keep writing until the feelings that were unclear have clarified or the stuck place has been recognized and, perhaps, become unstuck.

Flowing with Music ❀

Music is an important element in self-care. It can be a great source for inner peace, energy, and healing. You can listen to it while drawing, journaling, and moving your body. You can make music even if you've never tried before. It can be a source of fun and freedom.

Set aside the way you usually choose music to listen to, and, instead, consider all the many possibilities. As you search for music to support your self-care work, go beyond your personal likes and dislikes, even beyond what is familiar. What might help you open to self-care a little bit more? Listen to music from

> ✐ *Music is very nurturing. It is what I do when I'm not in touch with myself – I stand there with the guitar and I wait and see what comes out. –Leah* ✐

other cultures or ethnic groups and from unfamiliar styles. Look for music with which you can dance, draw, express feelings, and write. Try the following ways to enjoy flowing with music as you learn something new about yourself.

Draw with Music

All you need is a pad of newsprint paper (big paper can be fun to use), crayons or some other art media, and your music. What is your mood? Your body energy? What music do you feel matches your mood? Put the music on, and let it inspire your hands and fingers (or feet and toes!) to draw.

Journal with Music

Choose your music to fit your mood and energy. Do some steady, relaxing breathing to help you focus. In your journal, you might want to write about a particular topic, make a free-flow diary entry, or write a letter to a friend, relative, or yourself. After writing for a while, try a different type of music, and continue to write. Invite the music to bring you insight. Let your writing flow without judgment or editing. When you have finished writing, read your words out loud to yourself.

Musical Improvisation ✿

Whether or not you already play an instrument, let loose and enjoy the sounds that come from exploring music, simply for enjoyment's sake.

Materials:

Regular musical instruments that can be handled in a playful way, or create instruments from things you have around the house (like spoons, lids, cake pans, colanders, or trash cans).

Instructions:

Have some fun! Play with simple musical instruments. Remember to use your voice, too. Make music with all kinds of notes and all kinds of sounds. Try out a variety of instruments enjoying the unique sounds that each one makes. Then choose and get acquainted with one instrument. Play with it; get to know its individual spirit. The goal is to enjoy the experience.

Improvisation with Nature: A Conversation with the Natural World

Go outside with your instrument, and call out, sing, or play something to the natural world. Listen for a response. Continue to converse.

Copy a sound you hear in nature, and then keep on improvising. Enjoy how your sounds add to nature's symphony.

🍃

As you move on from your River journey, take a deep, refreshing breath. Imagine the variety of movements that a river makes, and feel the fluidity of those movements. Enjoy your ability to let the blocks to your creativity give way to your beautiful self-expression, just as the power of the river removes the dams of

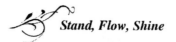

leaves and twigs. Movement and creative expression flow through you like the energized air that flows around moving water. Take a little time every day to tap into this wonderful energy. The more you get to know your creative energy by using it, the more at ease you will be with it. It holds great potential for you.

Shine Like the Sun

✐

The sun's glowing journey is a constant in our lives. It warms us when we are cold. Its consistent presence is reassuring. After days of clouds, we long to see it again. Its rising in the morning promises new energy, a new day. Its setting in the evening marks the slowing down of energy and the return of time to rest. Imagine that you can take the glow of the sun and put it inside you. Now imagine you are glowing from the inside out. From this center of light, move into your day.

This chapter on your self-care journey is all about letting your inner glow shine. You will be introduced to meditation, relaxation, guided imagery, and journal writing. These practices will increase your ability to focus, to create a relaxation response, to rediscover your imagination, and to connect with yourself in a new way. It takes a while to learn how to concentrate on an internal process and to see results. Be patient with yourself. When you take the time to set up your comfortable place and clear your calendar for just 20-30 minutes, you have already done something really terrific for yourself.

In this chapter:

Guided Relaxations

> Relaxing and Easing
> From Sensation to Relaxation to Healing

Mindfulness Meditations for Relaxation and Self-Care

> Sitting Mindfulness Meditation
> Walking Mindfulness Meditation
> Meditative Breathing
> Meditation of Connection and Gratitude

Reflections

> Relaxing Musical Journeys
> Journal Reflections
>> Morning and Nighttime Writing
>> Feelings Check-In
>> Everyday Gifts
>> Nurturing Yourself
>> Five New Comfort Activities
>> Treating Yourself with Kindness
>> An Interview with Yourself
>> Places of Reflection

These processes are excellent ways to develop your inner glow. You will want to find a comfortable and quiet place where you can walk, sit, or stretch out for several minutes. You can read the directions as you go along or record them and play them back to yourself.

Guided Relaxations

These relaxation processes will help you bring your attention to your body, use your focus to relax yourself, and create positive messages and images for you. Relaxation is the antidote to stress. Consciously taking time to relax can bring about healthy changes in your body. We offer two ways to guide you into relaxation. When you read them, let a gentle, rhythmic flow come with the words. You will find that you can call on these processes in times of stress to help you relax and come back to a place of centeredness and personal calm.

Find a quiet, comfortable place to sit or lie down. Loosen any tight clothing; take off your glasses and your shoes. Turn off phones and anything else that might disturb your concentration for the next twenty minutes or so. Let yourself be open and receptive. You are now ready to ease into relaxation.

As you read the following directions you will notice that the text is a continuous flow with (...) indicating places to pause.

Relaxing and Easing

Begin by paying attention to your breathing... breathing very, very slowly... in and out... Breathing in new, fresh air with each breath in... And letting it flow through you and out... New, fresh air flowing through you and out... Deep, slow breaths bringing nourishment to your body... Feel how good it feels to be nurturing your body with slow, deep breaths of fresh air... With each breath out, feel your body relax more and more... More deeply relaxed with each breath out...

Very slowly, begin to put your focus now on relaxing your feet. Begin to feel your feet relaxing and easing... Slowly feel your ankles relaxing and easing... Your lower legs relaxing and easing... Your upper legs relaxing and easing... Now your belly relaxing and easing... Ease any tension or tightness you may feel in your belly... Now around to your lower back. Your lower back relaxing and easing... And up your spine, vertebra by vertebra, relaxing and easing until you get to the top of your spine... Your neck now, relaxing and easing any tension or tightness you may feel in your neck... Your shoulders relaxing and easing... Loosening and letting go of any tension you may feel in your shoulders... Down your arms and into your hands, relaxing and easing... Your chest, relaxing and easing any tension or tightness you may hold in your chest... Back up to your face... Your jaw relaxing and easing... Your eyes, your forehead... Relax any tightness or tension... All the tiny little muscles in your face relaxing and easing... The top of your head, your whole head, relaxing and easing...

In your entire body, you feel a deep sense of calm and ease... In every muscle... Every limb... Every cell... Relaxed and eased... Pause for a moment... Feel the deep relaxation...

Now imagine yourself in a place that is special for you, a place that offers you comfort and calm. This may be a place you've been to before or perhaps it is new to you right now. This is a special place for you...

Begin to look around. Look at all that is around you. What do you see?...

Listen to the sounds, what can you hear?...

What textures are there? What can you feel?...

Perhaps there are some fragrances. What can you smell?...

Finally, there may even be something to taste. What can you taste?...

Be aware of how good your body feels right now in this special place...

Be aware of your emotions, your good feelings right now...

In addition to the feelings you've just noticed, be especially aware of feeling very calm and peaceful as well as strong and resourceful...

Most of all, feel a deep, deep sense of well-being...

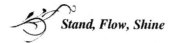

With this feeling of well-being, listen deep inside until you hear a message that is just what you need to hear right now: a message of reassurance and encouragement.

Listen for this message—a phrase or sentence. It could be something like this:

"I can relax now."

"I'm okay just as I am."

"I can do it!"

"I have what it takes to make it through."

Find your own words...

When you hear your special message, anchor it deeply inside yourself by breathing in very slowly and very deeply. As you slowly and deeply exhale, hear and feel that message deep inside...Do this slowly and deeply three times...

You now have the ability to calm yourself and relax. You can do this whenever you need to or want to. You can deeply relax your body. You can imagine being in a calming place. You can hear and anchor a message, a special message that comes from deep inside you...

Just rest in the good feeling you now have—the good feeling of relaxing and easing—and hearing your anchored message—as long as you need to...

When you are finished for now, say goodbye to your special place and your experiences there, and bring yourself back to the room where you began...

Gradually move your fingers and toes...Then your hands and feet...Slowly stretch out your arms and legs...Keep your eyes closed and, if you are lying down, turn over to one side and breathe in and out three times...Slowly lift yourself up into a seated position...

Now, ever so slowly, begin to allow light into your eyes as you open them...Sit for a few moments in this position, aware of how good it feels to be so relaxed...Thank yourself for taking this time to care for yourself in this way...

From Sensation to Relaxation to Healing

Begin by taking three deep breaths... Let these breaths be deep, cleansing breaths... Each breath helps you relax a little bit more...

Continue to use your breath to relax as you focus your attention on the sensations in your head and face... Notice if there is any tension around your eyes and in your jaw...

Now take a deep breath in and exhale... let your eyes, jaw, face, and head release any tension that may have built up there....

Let go of the tension; invite relaxation to flow all through your face and head...

Now move your focus to your neck and shoulders... Just as you did before, notice the sensations in this area... Take a deep breath in... And as you exhale, let any tension in your neck and shoulders go... Let the tension go completely...

Invite a feeling of relaxation to flow all through your neck and shoulders...

Now move your focus to your arms and hands... Notice any sensations in your arms and hands... Take a deep breath in, letting go of any tension as you breathe out... And as the tension flows away, invite a feeling of relaxation to flow all the way down to your fingertips...

Now you have relaxed your face, head, neck, shoulders, arms, and hands... Take a long breath in... And now let it go... Invite the relaxation to continue to flow through these parts of your body...

Now take your focus to your back... From your shoulder blades, down your spine, and outwards to your ribs, middle and lower back...

All the way down to the tip of your spine... The whole length of your back... Notice any tension that may be in your back... Take in a deep breath... And, as you exhale, let the tension in your back flow away... As the tension eases, invite a feeling of relaxation to come into every part of your back...

Now that your back is relaxed, bring your focus around to the front of your body, your central core... You may notice that your breathing comes easier as you relax more...

Focus on the front of your body from your collarbones to your chest, abdomen, and pelvis... Notice the sensations in these parts of

your body... Notice if there is any tension and take a deep breath once again... Give that tension permission to go, as you exhale... Take a second breath and relax your central core again... Invite relaxation to flow all through your core...

Now focus on your legs and feet... Notice the sensations... Note any tension... Take a deep breath once again... Give permission to any tension in your legs and feet to release as you exhale... As the tension eases, invite relaxation to flow all through your legs and feet...

Now return to the breath again. Take two or three deep breaths, slowly in and out, and connect all parts of your body with these breaths. Feel relaxation flow throughout your entire body...

Now let your imagination take you to the next step...

Begin to imagine a place that is your own healing room where you can be totally comfortable and totally yourself... Let your inner senses paint a clear picture of this place...

Are there windows and doors?...

How would this room be furnished?...

What colors and forms would you see there?...

Would there be any musical instruments or sound equipment?...

Would there be books and pictures?...

What do you like to do in this room?...

Now that you have created the image of your healing room, imagine that you can step into it and find yourself there, relaxed and at ease...

Enjoying the surroundings, find a place to settle in for a little while...

Perhaps you have a special need for healing today... Visualize or think about that need, and affirm that your special healing room is the best place you can be right now... Relax and invite the flow of healing energy to move all through you... Stay quiet inside, and invite any healing advice to come from deep within... Stay in this place for a while longer...

Now look around again at the scene, remembering it well... Anchor the image of this room by imagining a place within yourself where you can keep it... Perhaps it appears in a tiny version in your hands

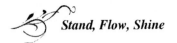

when you put your hands over your heart...Or perhaps when you breathe three slow, deep breaths, the image comes back when you invite it back...

When you have anchored this image, take three slow, deep breaths, and affirm that you now have a healing room within yourself. You can visit it whenever you need to or want to.

Now bring your awareness and attention back in this room and back to your body, relaxed and at ease. Feeling good...

Now that the guided relaxation has ended, gradually begin moving your fingers and toes, then your hands and feet, making gentle rotations...Cup your hands over your eyes for a while, and then open your eyes slowly...When you are ready, move your hands away...If you are lying down, gradually sit up...Notice how good you feel to have taken this time to relax.

By taking time every day to relax, you will go a long way toward restoring your emotional and physical balance.

Mindfulness Meditations for Relaxation and Self-Care ✿

When you take time to simply be, you will experience benefits that range from having less stress and worry to developing your self-confidence, creative energy, and inner peacefulness. Mindfulness meditation is a simple practice to focus your mind. When you quiet your mind with a focus on the breath, you have begun to meditate.

Sitting Mindfulness Meditation

Find a quiet time and place to sit on a cushion or chair with your back as straight as possible. Close your eyes or fix your gaze on a pattern in the floor or rug in front of you or on a small object like a stone, a flower, or a shell. Begin to clear your mind, imagining it to be like a still, quiet pond. Take some slow, deep breaths.

Pay attention to the rise and fall of your belly with each breath in and each breath out. Pay attention to the air flowing in and out of your nose. Try to follow this flow. You may want to say to yourself "Breathing in; breathing out" as a touchstone to follow and to bring you back from distraction.

Any sounds that you may hear—just notice and say to yourself "sounds." Go back to paying attention to your breathing. Any feelings or sensations you experience in your body—just notice and say "sensations." Follow the same pattern with thoughts that arise—note them as "thinking," and go back to paying attention to your breathing. When you catch yourself drifting, delight in catching yourself. Note it: "drifting." Go back to paying attention to your breathing – in and out.

If your mind wanders many times, bring it back just as many times. The more you are aware of your drifting, the more mindful you become. No judgment, just noting, and enjoying the calm, centered feeling. Mindfulness is about being aware, being present to the world around you and to yourself. It is a good way to practice *be*-ing.

Begin your meditation practice with a short sitting session of five to ten minutes. You can use a bell or a chime to mark the beginning and the ending of your meditation. Gradually build up your meditation time. If possible, sit and meditate for ten to twenty minutes a day. Beginning the day with meditation (even before you leave the bed) provides a base of both calm and energy. Any amount of time is valuable for becoming more mindful and relaxed. You can also use the practice in times of stress when you need a return to being rather than doing or trying to do.

To get started, here are some phrases you could try. (This is our variation of meditation phrases used by Vietnamese Buddhist teacher Thich Nhat Hanh.) You can find one that fits and just repeat it, or you can say each one three times. Then just pay attention to your breath. (You can also use these phrases whenever you need to relax and center yourself.)

> Breathing in: My mind is still.
> Breathing out: I am here.
> Breathing in: I am a serene woman.
> Breathing out: I am peacefully present.
> Breathing in: I am calm.
> Breathing out: I am relaxed.
> Breathing in: My heart is open.
> Breathing out: I smile.
> Breathing in, breathing out
> Breathing in, breathing out
> Breathing in, breathing out

At the close of your meditation, feel your gratitude for these moments of stillness and compassion for yourself. This sitting meditation can be practiced anywhere, even for a brief moment. Let it bring you back to your calm, peaceful self.

Walking Mindfulness Meditation

Walking meditation is a movement variation of sitting meditation. It can be a useful practice for those who find it difficult to sit still for long. When you do a walking meditation outside, you can open your senses to nature's sounds, smells, textures, breezes, and light. You can choose a familiar place in nature, turning a hike into a meditation, or use it on any walk you take.

Place your feet lightly and peacefully on the earth with each step. Let your feet inform you, with each step, of the harmony between yourself and the earth.

It is also useful to do a walking meditation inside in a clear space, barefoot, on a floor or carpet. You can create a path or circuit to follow.

You might begin with five minutes of meditation and increase it over time. You will come to know what works best for your meditation time. You can also vary your meditations: five or ten

minutes of seated meditation followed by five or ten minutes of walking meditation.

And so, to begin:

Very slowly lift one foot and step forward while slowly breathing in.

Then slowly lift your other foot and step forward again while breathing out.

Keep your concentration within—your breathing, your stepping.

Keep your eyes in a soft focus just ahead of your step. Continue in this way until your walking meditation ends.

Variation: With the first step, say to yourself "Breathing in" and then with the second step, say "Breathing out."

You may find a rhythm that easily falls into two or three steps with the in-breath and the same with the out-breath. Continue with the pattern of coordinating your step(s) with your breath. Keep your focus on each step, each breath. If your attention wanders, gently bring it back. No judgment. No worry.

When your walking meditation comes to a close, feel gratitude for your meditation practice. Notice how good you feel, and visualize yourself doing it again soon.

Meditative Breathing

Your breath is with you all of your life. These simple exercises can enhance your awareness of the healthy effects of breathing. Yoga breathing and abdominal breathing are good ways to refresh you in the middle of a busy day or a stressful time. There are many types of yoga breathing exercises. For a start, here are three good ones:

~ *Counted Breaths*: Breathe in to a count of four; hold to a count of eight; breathe out to a count of eight. Repeat. Continue for ten breaths. Gradually build up to forty breaths.

~ *Diaphragm Breathing*: Place your hands on your diaphragm (hint: above the belly button). As you breathe in and out, feel your hands rise and fall with the breath. Keep your shoulders still; keep your chest still. Focus on your diaphragm and your hands. Practice this daily. Practice in your car at stoplights, when you are on the phone, or as you wait in line. The next time you feel anxiety creeping into your body, start diaphragm breathing, and maintain it as long as possible. Practice will make the response come more easily when you need it. This breath technique is a natural anti-anxiety practice recommended by psychologists and yoga teachers alike.

~ *Three-Part Breath*: Breathe in, expanding and filling with air your belly, then your diaphragm, and then your chest. Breathe out, emptying the air from your chest, then your diaphragm, and then your belly. Continue for ten breaths. Gradually build up to forty breaths.

Meditation of Connection and Gratitude

This meditation process can help you feel more deeply connected with yourself, with others, and with the natural world. It can be done after some gentle movement processes, after meditative breathing, or at the close of your mindfulness meditation practice.

As you read the following sentences, find a gentle pace with your breath. Begin by taking a few deep, quality breaths in and out.

> Breathing in, feel a connection with yourself.
> Breathing out, feel gratitude for yourself.
> Breathing in, feel your connection with everyone you care about.
> Breathing out, feel gratitude for everyone you care about.
> Breathing in, feel your connection with all people everywhere.
> Breathing out, feel gratitude for all people everywhere.

> Breathing in, feel your connection with all parts of the natural world: the woods, the waters, and the wildlife.
> Breathing out, feel gratitude for all parts of the natural world.
> Now, breathing in, return to yourself, and feel an even deeper connection with yourself.
> Breathing out, feel gratitude again for yourself.

You can end this meditation by ringing a bell or some other lovely sounding object. Savor the feeling of connection as you go into the rest of your day. You can return to it at any time by taking a few deep breaths.

Reflections

When you take time to reflect on your self-care journey, you bring light to the subject of your attention. The sun's light reflects off the smooth surface of a lake, creating fascinating patterns. As it shines through the water, you can see the hidden treasures below.

These processes invite you to relax, move into your daydream consciousness, and experience your own inner glow. It is a place of letting go of worries and concerns to allow your own deeper wisdom to be tapped. You have experienced this place in the guided relaxations, the creative flow processes, and previous journaling activities.

Relaxing Musical Journeys

Every day your life has music in it. You hear it in the car, when you are on hold on the phone, at the mall, grocery store, and gym. If you play an instrument or sing, you know the wonderful experiences that can be had with music. This section begins with a process of listening to music that can take you on an inner journey.

Musical journeys are a good way to take a break from your ordinary routine and the tasks and stresses of your day. Let music

help you relax. Let it touch your emotions—happy, sad, joyful, angry. Let it take you within yourself to new levels of acceptance, compassion, and release. When you get to know your inner world, you may find that it holds many treasures, mysteries, memories, and feelings for you.

These instructions take you through a relaxation process that you give to yourself. You listen to a piece of music and let images and feelings come from within you. This journey is like a story. Set aside about twenty minutes for this process.

Find a piece of music to listen to. Music can help the imagery flow if it matches well with you and with what you need. You may want to spend some listening time to find music that will help you with this exercise. Here are some suggestions:

Pachelbel: *Canon in D*

Bach: *Sheep May Safely Graze; Air on a G String; Double Violin Concerto*

Vaughan Williams: *Fantasia on Greensleeves; Lark Ascending*

Holst: *Planets Suite: Venus and Neptune*

Satie: *Gymnopedies*

Massenet: *Thais,* "Meditation"

Japanese flute melodies

Harp music

New Age music with acoustic instruments

Soft piano jazz

Popular music and music with understandable lyrics may already have mental images you've attached to them, which can limit your response.

Relax. Begin the music as you relax. Take several deep breaths, following the rhythm of the music. With each breath, feel the air move in and out of your body. Imagine that you can follow it; your attention or point of awareness is moving in and out of your body with your breath. Now let your breath return to its natural rhythm. Take a survey of your body now. Start at your head, and notice how your head feels. If you become aware of tension, let the music help you let it go. Now move your focus to your neck

and shoulders. Gradually let your focus go to each part of your body. You may find that sometimes the tension moves away easily and other times it doesn't. Don't work at making the tension go. Simply return to a deep breath, let the music help you relax, and move on.

Think of an image. Now turn your focus from your body to your imagination. You may want to decide ahead of time what scene you wish to create. Perhaps the music suggests an image or scene. This is your time, your experience, so create something just for yourself. Here are some ideas:

~ Your favorite room or place in nature
~ An attic treasure chest
~ A gift you give to yourself
~ A sacred place where you feel a sacred presence

Once you have established the scene in your mind, let a story unfold as the music plays. Let yourself be involved with it. You need not judge what's going on. If you don't like how you feel, then you can choose to stop or change the experience. Let the story flow with the music as you stay focused on this inner experience. Enjoy experiencing the music and your imagination in this way. When you are ready, let the imagery fade, knowing that you can visit these images again.

Savor your experience. When you have finished your musical journey, take out your journal, and write down some of the images and feelings you experienced. You could also write about the music. This could be a good time to draw, expressing feelings and images through color and shape.

Journal Reflections

Writing down your thoughts, impressions, dreams, and inspirations not only makes you feel better but also can help you understand your innermost feelings and thoughts. Taking out your journal and letting words flow just for yourself can be a clarifying

and calming experience. You may also enjoy using your journal to reflect on your daily experiences as well as stories from your past.

There are many different choices for journals and journal keeping. You may want your journal to be like a scrapbook or an artist's journal, with sketches, clippings, and words. You may want a journal where you can easily tear out a page without disturbing the integrity of the whole book. You may want more than one journal, each with a different purpose: dreams, gratitude, creative inspirations, or daily reflections. If you prefer to write on your laptop or tablet, you may want to research journal writing software that will meet your needs. These may even include ways of keeping pictures and clippings.

Here are a few suggestions for shaping some journal entries. We encourage you to find time to start a journaling practice. It is time well spent.

Morning and Nighttime Writing

Writing in your journal when you first wake up will help you connect with yourself. As you make the transition from nighttime sleep to morning wakefulness, your dreams may be accessible. Write them down. Other thoughts and feelings that arise first thing in the morning can be recorded on the page.

Avoid using this writing time to make a to-do list. That can come later, when you are ready to get into the activity of the day.

Writing at the end of the day can be like putting yourself to bed. You can review positive experiences of your day and give yourself compassion for the difficult times. Use this time to gently close down the activity and energy of the day. You could write down some positive messages that you want to give yourself as you drift off to sleep. This is your "tucking in" time. This is your lullaby to yourself.

Feelings Check-In

This writing reflection is a good way to check in on your emotions. Begin by making time for yourself and creating a quiet setting.

This would be a good time to step into the sanctuary that you have created. Put on peaceful music, and have your journal or writing paper and pen ready. Center yourself by taking three slow, deep breaths, and then ask yourself, "What am I feeling right now?" Listen for the answer and then just begin to write. You may find yourself feeling a lot, maybe even crying. Or you may feel other emotions, like joy or fear or anger. Feel and write. Write and feel. Keep feeling; keep writing.

The next question to ask is "What are my deeper feelings?" As you answer this question, you could get to other feelings that need to be explored and given attention. Keep writing until you feel that you have come to an endpoint for now.

After you finish writing, read it all out loud to yourself.

Everyday Gifts

This reflection is an opportunity to take stock of the gifts that are in your life—the gifts you receive and those you give to yourself and to others. These gifts can be very simple things, such as how the sun greets you every morning, the neighbor's baby who smiles and coos at you, or the nap you take in a comfortable chair. Perhaps you treat yourself with a massage, warm shower, a fun movie, or a bit of chocolate. It is a shared gift when you reach out to others for company, conversation, a walk, or a hug.

To begin, center yourself with some slow, deep breaths. Close your eyes and contemplate the gifts in your life: the people, places, experiences, feelings, and things. After some moments of quiet consideration, open your journal. These questions can help you focus as you write about your gifts in your journal:

~ What are the gifts in my life right now?

~ What are the gifts I give to myself?

~ What are the gifts that I receive?

~ What are the gifts I give to others?

You can do variations of this journal exercise with different themes, such as gratitude, forgiveness, hope. Use the same questions, and just change the theme from "gifts" to something else.

Nurturing Yourself

This journal exercise can help you remember how important it is to nurture yourself. Once you feel the importance of taking care of yourself, then you probably will make more and more time to do so. Here are some questions to answer:

~ How does my body feel when I take the time to nurture myself?

~ What do I feel emotionally after I've taken good care of myself?

~ What do I notice in my interactions with others when I have given myself some self-care time?

~ Are there any changes at work or at home as a result of making myself a priority? What are they?

~ Then, once you recognize the benefits of nurturing yourself, you can answer the following questions:

~ What do I need to let go that gets in the way of nurturing myself?

~ What can I do that will be nurturing for me?

~ How will I go about making this change?

We have asked many women, "What do you do to feel nurtured?" Here are some of their responses:

I remember to do what calms me.

I take care of myself through prayer, meditation, and a daily workout.

I remember what makes me feel good: rest, taking classes, playing music.

I have found a community that I enjoy and find meaningful.

I cook good meals with good ingredients. I eat with no distractions.

I read good books, drink tea, and remember to breathe.

I take baths and get massages.

Five New Comfort Activities

Create a plan by thinking of five new comfort activities that you can do in the next five days to nurture yourself. Write these in your journal. Here are some activities you might try:

~ Give yourself a rest time each day, no matter how short.

~ Listen to relaxing music.

~ Wear a soft, comfy outfit around the house.

~ Take a leisurely walk outside.

~ Soak in a warm bath.

Read your whole list out loud every day for the next five days, and do your comforting activities. At the end of the five days, check in with yourself again. Keep on choosing comfort activities and doing them until nurturing yourself in this way becomes a habit.

Treating Yourself with Kindness

This reflection introduces an important practice for ongoing self-care. It starts with a journal reflection that helps you treat yourself with care and compassion.

✍ I believe in myself and whatever I'm doing. I just tell myself everything is going to be okay. I go ahead and do what I have to do and put love in everything I do! I love myself the best, and I take care of myself by loving myself, nurturing myself. –Lena ✍

Begin by asking yourself this question: "What does being kind to myself mean to me?" Write the answers in your journal.

Pause for a moment. Deepen your focus by taking three slow, deep breaths.

Picture being kind to yourself. Write in your journal about what this would look like.

Again, deepen your focus by taking three slow, deep breaths. Picture what may be standing in the way of treating yourself with kindness. Write in your journal.

Come back to deepening your focus by taking three slow, deep breaths. Picture how you will move past any obstacles on the way to being kind to yourself. Write in your journal.

Stand, Flow, Shine

One more time, take three slow, deep breaths. Now picture a specific situation where you are treating yourself with kindness. Feel the good feelings that come with caring for yourself in this way. Write about this in your journal.

Thank yourself for all that you do for yourself and all you have given yourself. Thank yourself for taking good care of yourself and taking good care of your body; thank your body for taking good care of you. Record all this gratitude in your journal.

Return to this reflection process whenever you feel the need to refocus your attention on being kind to yourself.

An Interview with Yourself

This journal process is a way to think about and record some key aspects of your life. The questions we suggest asking yourself are the ones we asked the women we interviewed for this book:
  ~ How would I describe my journey through my life; my life story?
  ~ What have been the challenges?
  ~ How have I taken care of myself?
  ~ What are the joys in my life?
  ~ What do I celebrate about being a woman?
  ~ What advice do I have for other women?

Places of Reflection ✿

With this set of processes, you are celebrating your creativity, connections with your own history, and your appreciation of nature. These reflections can be done as a whole set in a time put aside for self-care, or they can be taken one at a time when you want to do a bit of creative reflection. Suggested materials are listed at the beginning of each reflection. You can take some time to actually set up the reflection places and then begin with whichever

one you want, moving through them at your own pace. As you move through them, you'll take a mini-journey through different terrains of your world.

Haiku: All you need is your journal and a pen. Taking some quiet time, open your journal. Find an empty page. Close your eyes, and let an image, a thought, or a sensation come into your awareness. Now move toward the creation of a simple haiku poem. Here are the guidelines that govern a haiku: only three lines; five syllables in the first line; seven in the second; five in the third. Here is an example that fits this moment:

> *Allowing yourself*
> *To step out of time and space*
> *You compose a poem.*

If you want a little prompting, here are some possible themes for haiku:

~ Peace within
~ Intimacy
~ Self-care
~ Sweet moments
~ Gardens
~ Bridges
~ Living through crisis

Celebration: For this reflection, you need your journal and pen, music to listen or dance to, and a bubbly beverage or a special, tasty treat to eat.

What would you like to celebrate right now? Good friends? A comfortable day? Your health and well-being? A butterfly on your mailbox? See what you can come up with that is special for you right now. Put on some fun music. Make a toast to friends, butterflies, health—whatever!

Now sit down, and make a list of all the things you celebrate. Remember these things throughout the day, and keep the celebration going within yourself. Perhaps it will spill out to others and the party will evolve.

Ancestors: You'll need your journal and pen for this reflection, and you might also want to gather some family photos.

Where does your family come from? Do you know your family's history? This reflection could be a brief overview with broad brushstrokes. Or you may find that you want to dig back into some pictures, ask some questions, and do a little research. Think about what "ancestors" means to you. Write a family story in your journal.

A Child's Garden of Books: For this reflection you need your journal, a pen, and a favorite children's story or poetry book.

Perhaps, when you were a child, you were read to by a parent or grandparent. Perhaps you have read to your own children, nieces, nephews, or friends. Simple stories and rhyming poetry can be comforting at times of complexity. Find a favorite children's book, and read it out loud to yourself. What does it evoke for you? Write down your feelings, thoughts, and memories. Is a new children's story taking shape? Perhaps you can write one.

Nature's Inspiration: When you have an opportunity to spend some reflective time outside in nature, take your journal and pen with you. Feel the beauty all around. Seasons change, and nature remains. Is there an experience you have had with nature that inspired you in some way? Is there something special that you notice or know about nature? Write about your relationship with nature.

❧

With the sun as your guide, you have brightened your day in many ways. Just as the sun centers our solar system, so can your inner glow center you. The nature of our planet is a movement through light: to less light, to dark, to more light, to light again. The rhythms of your life move through these natural cycles. On your self-care journey, remember that natural rhythms occur, and that the sun and your own inner glow are always there and accessible to you. Slow down, breathe, and feel gratitude for the wonders of the universe that reside everywhere, including deep inside you.

Circles of Sharing

Imagine a smooth stone gently dropped into a still pond.
The ripples circle out, one after another. That stone is your commitment to your self-care. The ripples are the expanding positive effects that reach you and others you meet on your journey. As you feel your own center strengthening, you can connect with other women, and your caring spreads out to the wider circles each of you touches.

In this chapter we introduce you to a model for starting your own women's group: *a sharing circle*. We also suggest several activities that can be done in any group. A sharing circle can provide many positive benefits. These include getting personal support, having help focusing on your goals, finding a safe place to express concerns, and having fun. You may deepen existing friendships and develop new friendships based on caring, compassion, and encouragement for your self-care journey.

In this chapter:

Sharing Circle

Nurturing Activities

Ask For What You Need
Showered With Love
Encouragement

Playful Possibilities

Name Game
Spaghetti Knots
Group Juggle
Self-Care Suitcase
Group Empowerment Improvisation

Next on your priority list, just after making a commitment to your personal well-being, put finding time to be with friends. In a 2003 landmark study on friendships among women, UCLA researchers found that women deal better with stress in their lives when they have friendships they can turn to. Most re-

◆ I have lots of nice friends, and we are good to each other. We share our sorrows and our joys with each other and comfort each other.
–Lena ◆

search about stress, before this study, was with male subjects and articulated the primitive response to danger as fight or flight. This study found that a woman's natural response in times of danger was to tend to the children and gather with other women. Other studies have shown that women's friendships make women healthier, with fewer physical impairments and more joy in their lives.

In your own life, you may find that friendships have ebbed and flowed with your level of busyness. If you are a woman in the sandwich generation, taking care of children and parents, you may have very little time for friendships. Or perhaps you are in a primary relationship that demands your time and energy. You might be in school or in a career that requires your focus.

We encourage you not only to make time for friendships but also to come together with women in small groups to share your common interests and your personal lives—in short, your self-care journey. How good it is to be with other women who share mutual caring, trust, and respect for one another!

You are a part of a long tradition of women coming together in circles of sharing throughout the history of humankind. Jean Shinoda Bolen, a Jungian analyst, asserts that groups of women meeting together and sharing their love, vulnerabilities, and creativity have a healing effect for the whole planet.

This journey of self-care is not a solitary path. Every woman is eligible to be your sister. A fun night out could fit your needs right now. A lively

◆ I believe there is something very special about women. Women love to talk to each other and can be easily intimate with other people. Women want to know how relationships work.
–Marge ◆

book group may be what would excite you. You might feel most comfortable going into an existing group with professional leadership focused on a particular concern. Every community has support groups organized around health and behavioral topics such as chronic illness, weight loss, smoking cessation, and various twelve-step programs. Hospices have grief groups.

Marilyn:

When my husband was diagnosed with a terminal illness, the whole family was devastated. But we had to find a way to get through each day. One day, I had the thought: what I need and want are women to come to my house, to share food, and to hear my unfolding story. I put together a group of women from many different parts of my life. They came; they brought food; they laughed and cried with me. They listened and were my best support. We continue to meet. We love to get together as we all share a deep connection and caring for one another. This experience has taught me how essential it is to my well-being to meet with women to share, feel, and enjoy our lives together.

Sharing Circle

A *sharing circle* is the perfect place to practice unconditional caring for each other. This is an opportunity to give and receive caring attention, listen more deeply to yourself, and voice your thoughts and feelings in the safety of your group. Here you can ask for just what you need in the moment. You have a place to tell your story, to be heard, noticed, and listened to with caring and compassion.

To get your own group started, you could do some journal writing to help you focus on what is in your mind and heart. Think about who might be interested in coming to a group like this. Write down about six names, including your own, and let that list sit for a while. Perhaps when you look at it again in a few

days, you will make additions or subtractions to the list. When you feel ready, share your ideas about starting a group with these women, and ask them to join you in this adventure. It may take a while to find a mix of women who resonate together, but the benefits of forming a lasting group are worth the effort.

This group may take place in the members' homes or any place that provides closeness and quiet. A sharing circle can meet at whatever time interval works for everyone. Some groups meet monthly, while others come together as often as once a week or, if the women must travel to be together, as infrequently as once a year. It can be fun to include a potluck dinner or dessert.

Consistent attendance will strengthen the connection, depth, and trust in the group. When you know that your sharing will stay within the group, you will each feel safer to share your personal thoughts and feelings.

A wonderful way to get a group started is to introduce an activity that creates a sense of connection from the very beginning. Here is one way to do this:

Have a simple hoop (a grapevine or wreath from a craft store) and colorful yarn. Begin by tying one end of the yarn to the hoop. As each woman introduces herself, she takes a turn to transform the plain hoop into a colorful web by weaving the yarn around the hoop as she answers a few questions:

✐ I like that nurturing sense of compassion that women have. If someone is telling me something, I can picture it in a way that I can relate to them so they know they are understood. I like that. I celebrate that in other women: a sense of sisterhood and hanging together, not competition. I was a victim of mean girls when I was growing up, probably up until high school. Since then, I've always valued that sense of being close to somebody and almost having them finish your sentences, understanding. That's been good. —Susan ✐

~ What is your first name?
~ What are you feeling right now?
~ What would you like to feel when you leave?

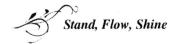

You can adapt the questions to your group's needs and goals. Pass the hoop around until you have all introduced yourselves. Establish a feeling of connection as you enjoy the beautifully interwoven web you have created.

You can use this hoop device each time you meet, adding more yarn loops with each gathering or removing the original yarn so that the hoop begins emptied of yarn each time. One of the group members can volunteer to be the hoop keeper.

Another way to begin a sharing circle is to use a smooth stone that fits comfortably in a hand. You can call this the *talking stone*. The group gathers in a circle and passes the stone from one woman to another as each person introduces herself.

The stone also focuses ongoing sharing. Place the stone in the center of the circle. When someone takes the stone from the center, it is her turn to speak. For the others, it is a time for deep listening from the heart, with attentiveness, caring, and acceptance. The stone is returned to the center of the circle after each woman speaks. Take a few moments, remaining silent, to honor what has been shared and to open the space for the next woman. This can be a caring experience for everyone!

Another simple focusing device uses the sound of a bell, gong, or Tibetan singing bowl (a small brass bowl that "sings" when the rim is touched with a wooden stick). One of these instruments can be used to begin and end a group meditation or other processes done with the group. These gentle ways of focusing attention help everyone stay present.

In a sharing circle, every woman takes a turn. She has the opportunity to share with the group what she wants the group to know about herself and what's been happening in her life (what she's been doing, thinking, feeling, reading) since the last group meeting. A woman might also use this time to share what is in her heart and mind at this particular moment. Or she may ask for something specific that she wants or needs, such as hugs, feedback, brainstorming, advice, or silence. At any time, a woman may choose to pass her turn.

Your group can explore many types of activities such as sharing concerns, being playful, meditating, and doing creative activities. All are good possibilities. You can adapt many of the activities in the previous chapters (Tree, River, and Sun) for your group's use. Look for this symbol: ✿. The energy that a group brings to those processes is different from what you experience when you do them alone.

At the end of your time together, have a closure process. It could be as simple as a short meditation, a song, or each of you offering a wish for the group.

The following circle processes and any of the other activities that we suggest for groups could be included in a sharing circle or could be incorporated into other settings where you gather with women.

Nurturing Activities

Receiving nurturing from a caring group of women enhances your self-care journey. Here are some of our favorite ways to nurture one another. Although we have suggested that each of you goes into the center for your turn, these activities can also be done while remaining within the circle.

Ask For What You Need

Your group stands in a circle. Each of you, one at a time, goes into the center of the circle and asks to be hugged, to be sung to, or whatever you each feel you need at the time.

Showered with Love

One at a time, each of you goes to the center of the circle and closes your eyes. The other women stand close and give love by holding their hands about three inches away from you. Silently they move their hands gently and slowly in a flowing motion as if

they are giving you a gentle shower. They repeat this motion two more times.

You stand still and receive this showering of love and caring. When the "shower" is finished, step out of the center, and let the next woman be showered with love.

Encouragement

As you begin, everyone in the circle takes a few deep, relaxing breaths. Listen inside yourselves for words of encouragement or reassurance that are just what you need to hear right now. Anchor this message deeply by taking a slow deep breath in, and as you slowly, deeply breathe out, hear the message inside. Feel it deep down inside yourselves. Open your eyes.

Each of you goes to the center of the circle, one at a time. Speak your own words of encouragement and listen as the others say those words back to you.

Anchor your own message again, taking in these words of encouragement and reassurance.

Playful Possibilities

Women love to laugh and have fun together. Here are a few games that are sure to lighten your spirit and release your playful self. They are non-competitive and draw on cooperation among the players. All of the games can be used with your sharing circle, as well as with family, friends, co-workers, and in other group settings.

Name Game

This game is a thoroughly enjoyable way to bring a group together.Each of you introduces yourself to the group in a way that is unique to you. Say, sing, chant, or shout your name. As you make the sound of your name, make a simple movement. Now

stay still, watch, and listen as everyone in the group echoes the sound and movement of your name back to you. Enjoy the feeling of being heard, echoed, and recognized. Each person in the group takes a turn.

Spaghetti Knots

This game is a reminder of how you get yourself "tied up into knots" and how you can help each other untie your knots. Form a circle. Reach across the circle, and take one person's hand with one of yours. Take another person's hand from across the circle with your other hand. Everyone should be holding two other persons' hands.

Now the task is to unknot yourselves without letting go of the hands you are holding and to form a circle again. You can reach high or low or even gently climb over others if necessary to undo the knot. Do whatever it takes to form a circle again, even if you have to temporarily let go of a hand you are holding or wind up facing backwards. Keep talking together, keep playing with it, and keep laughing.

Group Juggle

This game strengthens group connection while reminding each of you of the juggling that you do every day. Start by forming a circle. One person remains outside the circle throughout the game. She hands a ball (preferably a ball that is large and soft, like a beach ball) to one person in the circle. This person throws the ball gently to someone across the circle. (Underhand is usually best.) That person throws it to someone else across the circle who throws it to someone else across the circle. Keep this up until everyone has caught and thrown the ball. This is now your pattern.

Repeat the throwing pattern. The first person again throws the ball to the same person across the circle, and that person to the same one she threw it to before. Each person throws it to the

same person as before. Feel free to call out to the person to whom you throw the ball to let her know that it's coming.

The person outside the circle then adds another ball, giving it to the first person in the group to throw. After a while, another ball is added, and another, and then another, depending on the size of the group and the number of balls you have. (Three to five balls are usually enough. Any more might be overwhelming!)

Continue as long as you want or until the person outside the circle takes one ball out at a time until no balls are left. Enjoy the laughter and the fun.

Self-Care Suitcase

What really takes care of you? Do you wish you could remember to take care of yourself wherever you are? This game helps you remember your self-care in a whole new, playful way. It is like the childhood game: "I'm going on a trip and in my suitcase I'm going to pack _____." This variation is: "I'm going on a trip and in my self-care suitcase I'm going to pack _____."

Sit in a circle. One of you begins by saying "I'm going on a trip and in my self-care suitcase I'm going to pack _____." Fill in the blank with a self-care practice, such as *"yoga."* Use a gesture to show what you are packing.

Then the next person says the phrase, repeats what you said and your gesture, and adds her own. For example: "I'm going on a trip and in my self-care suitcase I'm going to pack *yoga and playfulness.*"

The third person continues the pattern: "I'm going on a trip and in my self-care suitcase I'm going to pack *yoga, playfulness, and meditation.*" And on and on until everyone in the group has packed her self-care suitcase.

Making a gesture to demonstrate what you are packing helps others remember your item when it's their turn to "pack their suit-cases." As you go along, everyone can help each other out by giving hints and showing their gestures.

Group Empowerment Improvisation

This is a creative group process that develops around the theme: *Empowerment*. The exercise can be done by dividing a group into smaller groups (even twos or threes if necessary). When the groups have been formed, you spend time together creatively solving the group task: to come up with a series of movements, a skit, a song, or a human sculpture that would show the other group what it would look like to feel fully empowered. Take about ten minutes together to brainstorm and rehearse. Then each group presents its "performance." Applause, laughter, and appreciation are given freely to each performing group. Your group can also do this together as one group with the same instructions and enjoyment.

Any topic could be chosen for this group creation. Here are a few suggestions: peacefulness, joy, or wisdom.

Here are some comments from women's sharing circles to inspire you as you start your own circle:

A moment and place in time with this wonderful, giving, strong circle of women.

I enjoy the safe and nurturing environment and being able to speak and be heard.

I enjoyed every moment where we could hear stories from each other directly about experiences and lessons learned.

I smile so much it hurts. I love laughing with these beautiful women.

I really appreciate the encouragement, bonding, and communication with other women.

I like being quiet with women and sharing feelings.

I enjoyed laughing, crying, being with such an accepting group, and the feeling of support. We all have our stuff.

 *Stand, Flow, Shine*

Expanding circles radiate across a pond touching other circles. They overlap; they resonate with one another. Your circle is like this. Your life journey is enriched by connecting, sharing, listening, respecting, and having fun with other women. You share the joy of sisterhood and common experience. Your circles become one, and you can enjoy the bliss of being held in this wonderful Circle of Sharing.

Continuing Your Journey

We are so glad that you have joined us through these pages.
As you think back over what you have experienced with this book,
imagine for a moment or two that you are leaning against a tall,
sturdy tree, feeling its enduring presence, mindful of its ability
to adapt to changes that happen through its lifespan. Nearby, the
sound of flowing water draws your attention to a stream. You
see that it flows around boulders, carries twigs and leaves with it,
and invites you to refresh and renew yourself. Warm sunshine is
shining through the leaves offering relaxation as you close your
eyes and breathe deeply.

In this book, you have learned how to take care of yourself
and make yourself a priority in your life. We especially hope that
you have discovered and strengthened your ability to relax, renew,
and empower yourself. We happily support and encourage the
continuation of your self-care journey.

We offer you a final visualization process for deepening your
inner wisdom and well-being. We end the visualization with messages of encouragement for your journey forward shared by other
women on their self-care journeys.

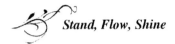

Rainbow Meditation

🖥 Find a comfortable place to sit or lie down, and cover yourself with a blanket or shawl for further comfort.

Begin to pay attention to your breathing, taking in a slow, deep breath and letting it out slowly and deeply.

Again, a slow, deep breath in, feeling new fresh air flowing through you and out.

One more slow, deep breath in—relaxing more and more deeply as you slowly breathe out.

Now imagine that you are outside this room. A breeze comes and gently lifts you up. Relax as you are carried with comfort and care.

You see before you a beautiful rainbow with the colors red, orange, yellow, green, blue, and purple. You are gently carried to that rainbow.

You enter the red of the rainbow. Here, you are free from fear. You feel safe. You feel like you belong. Take in the healing color red.

Feeling safe and free from fear, you enter the healing color orange, where your emotions can flow freely.

Feeling safe, emotions flowing freely, you enter the healing color yellow, where the heat of the sun burns away any obstacles that keep you from being who you want to be.

Feeling safe and free from fear, emotions flowing freely, feeling free to be who you want to be, you enter the healing color green and feel your heart open; you are filled with unconditional love for yourself and all others.

Feeling safe and free from fear, emotions flowing freely, being able to be who you want to be, your heart open and filled with unconditional love, you enter the healing color blue, where any tightness or tension in your throat space is released and you are able to speak your truth.

Feeling safe and free from fear, emotions flowing freely, being able to be who you want to be, your heart open and filled with unconditional love, able to speak your truth, you enter the healing color purple, where you feel peace so deep it's beyond words.

Feeling safe and free from fear, emotions flowing freely, being able to be who you are, your heart open and filled with unconditional love, able to speak your truth, and filled with deep peace.

You are slowly carried further by the breeze and gently placed down in a beautiful meadow full of wildflowers. You notice a path before you, and walking slowly toward you along this path is a wise woman...

She tells you that she is here to offer you a gift, a message of support and encouragement for your journey ahead in your life. She leans down and whispers this message in your ear...

Listen carefully... And then anchor these words of wisdom deeply inside by taking a deep breath in and then hearing and feeling this message deep within as you slowly, deeply breathe out. Repeat this two more times. You thank the wise woman, knowing that you now have the gift of her wise words, her support and her encouragement, deeply anchored within you.

The wise woman walks back down the path, leaving you in the beautiful meadow. Again, a breeze gently lifts you up, and you are slowly carried back through the sky.

You begin to see below you the place where you started. It gets closer and closer as the breeze gently carries you down and back.

Slowly be aware of being back in this room, and rest for a while.

When you are ready, very slowly open your eyes, letting in the light little by little.

Move your fingers and toes.

Gently stretch your arms and legs.

If you are lying down, roll over to one side, take a few deep breaths, and slowly sit up...

Sit for a while, and feel yourself filled with the healing colors of the rainbow and the wise woman's message of support and encouragement. You can carry these within you on your path, your journey ahead, as you move forward with your life... *

---

*We thank Gina Sager, a mindfulness meditation teacher and healer, for her healing rainbow imagery that we have adapted here.

Here are some words of encouragement for your journey ahead that have been shared by other wise women:

~ Trust your heart.

~ You are perfect just as you are.

~ You deserve to be happy.

~ Find your bliss, and follow it.

~ You are loved.

~ You are beautiful and strong.

~ You can do this.

~ You are a talented and loving woman with lots of gifts to share.

~ Keep your heart open, and everything will be all right.

 *Stand, Flow, Shine*

We wish you a life of gentle inner peace. We hope that you continue to deepen your connection with yourself and that you treat yourself with care and compassion. As you travel ahead on your self-care journey, may you joyfully...

Stand Tall Like the Tree
Flow Like the River
Shine Like the Sun

Judith and Marilyn

WOMEN'S STORIES

Women's Stories

At each stage of a woman's life there are challenges and joys, struggles and accomplishments, loves and losses.

Throughout this book, we included comments from women we know who have walked this journey of self-care. They come from many different backgrounds and range in age from a high school senior to a centenarian.

When we interviewed them, we invited each woman to share her life journey, particularly how she has taken care of herself throughout her life. We asked what she feels is unique about women and what she wants other women to know. In the following pages, you will find a few of their stories.

Although all the women we interviewed shared wonderful, inspiring stories, we could not include each one here, and the stories that are here are slightly edited for length. You will find the stories of all the women we interviewed on our website: www.StandFlowShine.com. We are grateful for their deep and thoughtful reflections, their humor, and their candidness. We celebrate them, their life journeys, and their generosity in agreeing to be part of this self-care journey adventure.

As one of these beautiful women said, "I wouldn't want to be anything but a woman. Deep fullness and caring…nobody else can take a woman's place, and that's what I believe. Who else but a woman can do what a woman does?"

The Young Woman

A young woman experiences a sense of exploration and freedom, as well as the challenges and stresses of forming relationships and learning to depend more on herself. Learning to relax and find her own abilities and strengths will solidify her journey into adulthood.

Sarah

Sarah (19) is concerned about issues of social justice and human rights. She plans to be a social worker to use her caring and compassion to help others.

My life journey has been unique in that I've traveled a lot, and I've moved between countries. Growing up between England and New Jersey has definitely shaped me.

My parents got divorced when I was five or six years old, and I was living in England. It actually didn't seem that big a deal at the time. I was excited because it meant that I would move to America. I was like, "Hollywood, Disneyland," and all of those types of things.

Because I was young, it was kind of an advantage. It was just the way things were. I love my father very much, and I definitely missed him, but I adapted pretty easily.

I had a lot of mental health problems when I was a younger teenager. When I was thirteen to fifteen, I was very depressed. I had anorexia. I did some drugs and drinking and all of that stuff. I had a few hospitalizations. It was a very difficult time, and I wouldn't wish to relive it or to have anybody else live through it.

It's definitely made me a stronger person, and it's given me a lot of perspectives that I wouldn't have otherwise. It's given me a lot of empathy towards other people, a lot of understanding of mental health problems and the stigma around people who have them. Sometimes when I tell people about my struggles in the past, they are like, "Oh, I would never have expected you to have been through that!" I think, "What do you expect people who've had mental health problems to be like?"

The way I met my challenges was really deciding what I wanted in life. It had gotten to a point for me where either I really do something for myself and I fight this depression and I overcome it or I let this continue. I was determined that I could make myself better.

My father let me start fresh in England. I think this was very, very important for me. He said, "I respect you and trust you. If you want to get better, you can get yourself better." So it's pretty much what I did. I was very trustworthy.

It was hard, but I worked through that by trusting, respecting, and appreciating myself. I learned if I have enough strength to try to destroy myself, then I could reverse it. So, for example, if I could control myself enough to not eat properly and be anorexic, then surely I could use that self-control to say, "Well, I won't smoke pot, or I won't do drugs."

I am also a queer woman, somewhere between a lesbian and "bi." I came out when I was fourteen. I have dated a lot of really great girls and had great relationships. I think it definitely added some stress, especially in a society where gay marriage is this big, scary thing. But it's really about people loving each other.

I take care of myself by listening to myself. When I'm tired, I go to sleep, or when I'm hungry, I eat. When I'm stressed out, I'll take the time to sit back and relax or call my friends and meet them. I think a lot of it is just trying to get in touch with my own body and its indicators of whatever I need emotionally and physically.

Even when I'm lazy and tired, I see my friends. They are like, "Come on, feel the joy!" Surrounding myself with people who are positive is a very important part of taking care of myself. I also really enjoy listening to other people and helping them. Those are probably my favorite things to do.

I think everything is special about women! Caring, strong, intelligent women are the ones I tend to surround myself with. There is definitely solidarity among women—or at least there should

be—from sharing experiences and also from often being marginalized in society.

I would like other women to know that it is important to have confidence and strength in yourself. Keep a positive perspective and surround yourself with good, compassionate people. Keep the goodness and compassion in yourself and also share it with other people.

The Working Woman

A working woman may find the grind and stress of her career almost overwhelming. She is challenged to feel free, creative, and productive while at the same time juggling her relationships, responsibilities, and self-care.

Aisha

Aisha (28) is an energetic young woman who is in college and working full time at an integrative medicine center.

I grew up in the projects in Washington D.C. We didn't have that much money. My mother was on welfare for several years. I know how hard it is to live day by day where you've got people selling drugs.

My father was an alcoholic, so I grew up in a lifestyle that was not stable. He died of AIDS when I was thirteen years old. Before he died, I made a promise to him that I wanted to help people. My journey started with that promise to my father. I have fulfilled that promise. I try to give as much as I can. If somebody needs me, I'm there for you.

It took me a long time to graduate college, but I always knew that that's what I wanted to do. I started mentoring and tutoring through my church. We would get all the kids together. We helped them with their homework. I helped this little girl who was probably about 11 years old. I went to a play that she was in after school. She saw me there. Taking that extra little step helped

her, and it just made me feel a lot better. My mother couldn't do this for me because she was working all these jobs to make ends meet. It was the same thing with this girl. She had siblings she was taking care of, and her mother was working endless jobs. She didn't have that extra support. Just to see Miss Aisha come into her life, sit there in the audience, she was so happy. At the end of the year, her grades went up.

We didn't grow up with a computer. I didn't have Internet in my home because I couldn't afford it. It took me a lot longer to do things. I would sit in the library and look through the filing cards to try to find my book. I didn't know you do the search in the computer. And this was just a few years ago!

I've learned that it is important to take care of yourself because then you won't have a breakdown. I put a lot of energy into other things and forget about myself. So when I get overwhelmed, it's really at that tipping point where the anxiety and stress and stuff happen. When I was at school full time and working full time, I lost weight; I wasn't eating properly. I lost sleep. I was really a zombie. I was sick. I just kept going.

I finally thought to myself, "You work at a wellness center, Aisha. Why aren't you taking advantage of this?" Well, I don't have time. "Well, you need to take time for yourself." So for a graduation gift for myself, I got an acupuncture treatment. It was the best thing I could have done. I try to get an acupuncture treatment once every two months or so to help out with that anxiety that I have.

My mom is the very first joy in my life. She is just a doll. I love that lady. She is so supportive. Other joys are my cat, my degree, completing school. I'm blessed and thankful that I'm not the product of my past environment. My grandmother is also a big joy to me.

I celebrate being a woman. We are powerful. If it weren't for us, doggone it, folks wouldn't be where they are today. I don't have any kids, so I don't know the experience of having kids. But

the fact that a woman can produce a child is a pretty awesome thing.

We get more respect than my grandmother did or even my mom did. I still don't think we're equal, but we're up there. I enjoy that. I enjoy the challenges of being a woman because I like to prove them wrong.

The other thing that I celebrate about being a woman is the nurturing and understanding that we have. We have extra feelings, I think. You can ask a man, "How do you feel?" "Okay." If you ask a woman the same thing, it's "Oh, goodness, I feel this and this..." And they'll come up with all these different things, and you really get a sense of who they are. We're just unique; we're beautiful; we're powerful. We have a voice now.

The advice I have for other women is that it can be hard and frustrating, but as long as you have faith, you can get through any obstacle that comes in your direction. Faith is believing in something. We go through a lot, and people test our trust, our values. But you still have to have trust.

As long as you carry trust in yourself through your journey, you're going to be all right. If you have somebody who tries to put you down and says that you can't do it, you say, "No! I can do it!" Only you know what you can do.

Pat

Pat (58) is a dedicated paralegal and a gifted potter. She has always been committed to efforts for peace and social justice. She has two grown children and one granddaughter.

In my journey through life, there is a marker around sixteen. I feel like I had, up until then, a pretty insulated and not very good life inside my family. At sixteen, I began to make some new and different friends who really showed me the door to get released from the experiences in my family. It was through friendships with two women that I connected with the civil rights movement, the antiwar movement, and later, feminism.

Earlier, I had been running full speed into lots of dangerous situations, lots of hitchhiking, and just on this rush to have experiences. I did not exactly know why and did not really have any way to make sense of them. I felt as though I was a rock hurling through space.

I adopted my first child as a single parent, and then, five years later, I had a child with a partner. Through being a mother, I connected with lots of parts of myself. I think that allowed a sort of reintegration of aspects of myself that were pitched about in that "hurling decade." I began to reorganize and to really begin an adult life that began to make more sense.

As I'm getting older, I'm more patient with other people who are different from me and how they process and experience their lives. I'm in less of a rush to get people to arrive at some point that I'm at or to a destination that I think is important.

I have two kinds of work that have lots of meaning to me. One has social justice aspects to it, and the other is creative work. My full-time work is with families who have children with disabilities. I'm a paralegal, and I work with these families as they try to get their legal rights protected for their children's education. I work mostly in Baltimore in a small office filled with smart, progressive people who are quite diverse racially. I've been there for twenty-eight years, so it's really my life's work. It's been a great fit for me.

My other work is making pottery that I've been doing now for forty years. I like to make functional things with clay that other people can use and enjoy. It sort of goes back around for me. They think of me when they drink out of cups and bowls. I feel I get a little hit of good energy out of that. It makes the day brighter. I also make urns for people's ashes, and that is pretty amazing, too. It gives me a lot to think about.

I'm a serious person. I'm not waiting until everything feels real light and joyous, because that's not who I am. That's okay with me at this point. I do have a lot of fun, though. It doesn't

take a lot to make me feel like something is good. I'm lucky for that.

My granddaughter, who is five, is an enormous joy in my life. My children, as they are growing up, are a stupendous joy. My new loving relationship is a great and huge source of joy. Long-term friendships are unspeakably wonderful. Moments of feeling we are making some kind of dent in the terrible conditions of the world around us are really big joys. There aren't enough of those moments, but they are big.

The biggest challenge for me has been recovering from sexual abuse by my stepfather. It has taken lots of individual therapy work, group work, and tons of work with myself to recover from that. That has given me a way of understanding other people's experiences, which has been really important in my own work.

Another challenge is, as a white person in a society as complicated as ours, sorting out issues of class and race. Having a mixed-race family, I get very personal understandings of racism and how that works.

There have been other very interesting and driving challenges having to do with being a woman, understanding sexism and how that works. Spending time in relationships with women gave me the experience with how it feels to be on the outside of the heterosexual culture.

Getting to be, occasionally, in some exquisitely beautiful natural environments helps me deal with all these challenges. Exercise is something I always do to take care of myself, and that helps me tremendously.

Finding a way to make a life that has meaning and coherence has meant positioning my life in a way that had fewer contradictions in it. When there is a thread through work and where I live and how I live and who I live with and how I do anything, shop or cook, I feel much better. I've worked hard to do that, and that's been really significant. I think of the early labor song "Which Side Are You On?" The side I'm on is really to be connected with working people who are putting one foot in front of the other each day

to make a path, to make a living, and to make the world a better place. I think that captures what I mean.

I heard an interview with two characters from a play, one playing Martin Luther King and one playing Malcolm X. There was a question about the role of women in the civil rights movement. One of the actors said, "If you teach a man something, you've taught one person. But if you teach a woman something, you've taught lots of people." And I thought it so accurately captured this quality of connectedness that we seek out as women. There is an imperative to extend ourselves into each other's lives.

My advice to other women would be to have some close connections with women, slightly older, who aren't members of their own family. I've been able to play that role for some of my children's friends in a way that has been helpful for the younger person and for me. A younger friend of my son's was extremely lost. It was easy for me, as I wasn't her mother, to map some things out with her and to help her be accountable to the decision she was making. Maybe that's a mentoring role.

I think it's crucial, as we are making our way through our personal lives, to see them in the big context of humankind. To feel connected to yourself and then to others moves us all forward. I don't think we can really save our individual selves unless things get better overall.

The Mother

A mother is challenged to hold on to her sense of identity and well-being in the face of demands from her role as a nurturer of others.

Laura

Laura (33) was trained in social work and has taken a break from work to raise her little boy. She is an active volunteer in his school. She is personable and engaging and a sensitive, supportive mother and friend.

Having grown up in the '80s and '90s, when Women's Liberation had already happened, there was an expectation, I guess, that we go to work and have a career. What is interesting, now that I have a child, is that I think the women's movement is about doing whatever you feel comfortable with. So if you want to work, work. If you want to have children and stay home with them and are able to, do that. There is no pressure to be like a man or work like a man. I don't feel a lot of judgments about my decisions to work and then not to work as a new mother.

I am more content now that I am in my thirties. I was doing more searching in my late twenties and feeling really discontent, having expectations about how an experience should be and getting wound up about that. Whether that's been school or jobs or relationship with a partner, that's been hard. When I first got into my committed relationship, I was worried about losing my independence. I think I also had self-esteem issues about work.

Over the years, I've learned about making compromises. Now I don't really feel I have my niche in my career, but I also feel it's not breaking me apart. I'm just going to find my way, even if I have a new path or a path that is stopping and starting a little bit more than others.

The joys in my life are parenting and partnering, developing friendships, and revisiting relationships with my family. Connecting with people who are mothers or parents has just been a whole new world opening up. Mothering is a spiritual thing.

Being a mother to a very sweet, joyful little boy is fabulous! He brings a lot of energy. He is also very cuddly and snuggly. His little body is so sweet. He loves exploring things and finding games. He doesn't get bored just creating things. He has that sense of wonder in the world, and I feel like I'm going through that again. Why did we stop getting so excited about slugs or droplets of water on a leaf or raspberries? It's fun to learn how to explore the world again. I just want to be more in the present, in the Toddler Way.

Being a mother has also been a paradigm shift. I am blown away by how much it has taken over my life. It is a big loss of independence just having a baby, not being able to do what I want to do. I didn't really feel like I was prepared for that. It is all-consuming for me as a mother, at times. I feel overwhelmed with love. It's also been anxiety provoking, like "Oh, am I doing a good job, or are we doing a good job? Do we have enough resources for him?"

I try to check in with my own needs and see if they are being met, and then see what I can do about those things. I try to let go of expectations or worries because they're not very helpful. I'm learning to make myself okay in situations where I'm really challenged. It is important for me to stay connected to people and to try to share what's going on. I try to spend quality time with my family and my women friends. I usually get exercise and do some kind of connecting and grounding exercises, like yoga or meditation. Another way I take care of myself is by being in nature. Being very grounded with the earth, whether that means dancing or gardening, brings me a lot of joy.

I celebrate so many generations of grandmothers and great grandmothers and the strength that has come through to carry on living. A lot of that is working hard, cleaning house, baking bread, and making a home. Then, also, there are relationships between women: the intimacy, the friendliness, checking in, and being present for each other.

I'd like other women to know that it is important to trust your insights in dealing with yourself, and it's important to stay connected. It is so helpful to have women friends at every stage—high school, college, and after college. Learning how to be a better friend, supporting, getting support, learning how to give and receive, these are all important parts of a woman's journey.

Sophie

Sophie (late 30s) is in the midst of the busy life of a mother, wife, and graduate student. She manages it all with practicality and acceptance.

My journey through life has been full of surprises. Every time I say I don't want to do something or go some place, that seems to be right where I go. I never wanted to go to America from Australia, and here I am. I always knew I wanted to have kids, but I never knew how great it would be for me. That was a big surprise. I thought it was going to be a burden, really hard. I had that sense of it. But I didn't have the sense of how much fun it would be, and how great it would be to watch little kids grow up.

In work, it's not like a one-foot-in-front-of-the-other thing. You just take the opportunity, and it takes you in a different direction, a different path. I never would have thought I would become a librarian, but living so far away from Australia has really gotten me into technology and the library.

My children are growing up in a world that I don't have a whole lot of control over. I want them to be a part of the world that they are going to live in. I want them to be able to survive that. I try to help them find value in things that are not material: doing a lot of reading, playing in the grass and the trees, being down by the stream for four hours. That's a major challenge right now, keeping them grounded and nice people, peaceful people.

A frustration in my life is the division between my husband's life and my life, which I think a lot of women my age are feeling. The women are much more at home and with the kids. My challenge is trying to gracefully make a piece of time for myself.

So that's where I am, readjusting the roles and trying to figure out how that all works. Trying to find a little bit of space to be able to grow myself. Trying to do pieces of things. Getting back into working out. Trying to find ten minutes to have a cup of tea. Mammoth! I realize that you do really need to take care of yourself, even though you think you can live without, which you do for a very long time when you have infants.

My biggest way of taking care of myself is not wearing shoes. I love going outside in the morning and having my tea and putting my bare feet on the ground, no matter how hot or how cold it is. It grounds me. Walking out on the dew, just right there.

I think women are incredible. I celebrate the fact that women can be so incredibly patient, selfless, and powerful. To see what my friends can do when a child is sick, not even their own child, or when one of their friends is not well or needs them. Women are just so incredibly powerful that way, the bonds they can make and how they pull together on such a real level.

It amazes me that women have that power, such strength, to be able to work, have a family, a husband, and try and juggle it all. It's amazing. It's amazing that it doesn't just fall apart. I see my friends around me as the glue that really sticks communities together and sticks society together. It's not that they are all perfect. That's what I celebrate about women.

I'd like other women to know that they need to not give themselves a hard time, not be self-critical, and to realize that it's okay to just get it done. It doesn't have to be perfect. Just do what you can, the best you can. When you can't do it, just say you can't. Let it slide off your back and not beat yourself up about it. It's a tough act, being the glue and all. We all need to be a bit kinder to ourselves.

The Woman at Midlife

A woman at midlife faces the challenges of new roles, possible losses, and a changing body. She has much to celebrate as she settles into her own sense of self. A challenge for her is to develop a feeling of self-empowerment and strength through all these transitions.

Joyce

Joyce (54) is originally from Jamaica, West Indies. She works as a home health aide for the elderly. She loves to sing and dance,

and she brings enthusiasm and cheer to everyone she encounters.

I don't call this my heart story; I call it my *story heart*. My story didn't have a heart before now. My story was buried deep inside. There was no "alive" to it, no meaning to it. Talking about my life gives it a heart. I wish to share my story with you.

My mom and dad were peasants, farmers, in the south of Jamaica in Trelawny Parish. There were fourteen of us kids growing up. We were living way off the main, no roads, no nothing. We were so poor that my sister and I would go to the cornfield and get those hairs from the corn. Then we would get some cloth, shape it, put the corn hair on it, and that would be our doll!

One Christmas we were so sad. Everybody else was so happy, and they had Santa Claus coming around in a big truck, you know. But we were so far away, and we had to do our chores. We were hurrying up to get our work done so that we could go the four or five or six miles, run all the way there to see Santa.

We heard the bells and the announcement that Santa is coming through, and we ran and ran and ran. We got there, and Santa was gone! All the little kids that were living close by, we know they got their presents and their candies. They were just making fun of us saying, "Oh, the little kids from the bush, they didn't get anything." We cried all the way home.

The next morning my brother and I went to the river to get some water. There, in a big tree over the water, was a whole bunch of balloons. I called my brother and said, "Look in that tree, look what we got. We got our Christmas present!" Balloons were there for everybody! It was the best Christmas we ever had. We wished that little kids all over the world would have the same thing we had. So those are the little things that we really look back to, and we appreciate life more for what we have.

Sometimes I get so sad to know that my mom couldn't read us a story. She could not read. She could not even sign her own name. She said she went to school maybe one time in her lifetime. Her mom could not afford it, and her dad did not want her to go to

116

school. That's why she emphasized to us to go to school. But it was hard. Sometimes we would go to school without eating, without any breakfast, without any lunch. . No books, no pencils, nothing. We would go and maybe borrow books or go without books at all, because at that time books were very expensive. My car now, it's all packed up with books. I collect all the books I can get to take home to the little children there whose parents cannot afford to send them to school.

Being a woman is very challenging. I became a woman at fifteen years old, taking care of my cousins. Being a woman is not only being a female but being nurturing. I love caring for others. Sometimes we put ourselves aside and put others in front of everything. We need to nurture ourselves as well.

A big challenge that I faced was being a single mother. I saw my mother and how she really struggled to raise fourteen children, so I said to myself, "I have only three." I got a lot of inspiration from her. I was determined, and I did whatever I could to really take care of them and made sure that they had a good education. It was difficult, but when you do things out of love, it makes a difference, you know? I said, "Okay, well, today is here. I have to take care of today and make the best of it and do what I can to overcome all the obstacles, you know, all the different things." Sometimes you get so discouraged.

I take all my challenges with laughter and with happiness. Encouraging other people, I find satisfaction in that. When I am having difficult times, I go weep with a friend. They might be having the same problem, and I say to them, "Look, we can do this together. We can overcome our challenges if we really stick together."

Through all of the challenges in my life, I face them with hope and a determination that I am not going to let the past control my future. There is nothing wrong in looking back, even if you want to cry. By looking back, you are more determined to go toward the future. That is what I have learned. So each day I challenge myself to work a little harder. Sometimes, when things go wrong,

I count to ten. I breathe in and out, and I relax. I used to jump across the river. I said to myself, "This is a jump for you, if you can jump from one side of the river to the other. You can't swim. If you take that challenge, you can overcome whatever obstacle. Just keep jumping over, and try not to fall."

What really, really gives me joy in my life are my three children. I have three girls. I didn't get a boy! Then came along two grandsons. They are my world. They make me happy. There are some days that I feel like, "What's life all about? Forget life! Let me just lay down and die." And then I think, "Don't you want live to see your grandkids and your children grow up and see what they are going to be?" Those are the things that really keep me going. And friends, wonderful friends.

I love what I do! I am a nursing assistant, and I take care of the elderly. They have become like children, and I love children. It is up to you, within your heart, to think about all the things they are going through. You have to be able to live in their world, to see and to face the unknown of their world. I try, as best I can, to get into their world and encourage them and let them know that it is okay. Life is good. Life is a challenge. Life can be lonely. But look back on all the things they have had: their wonderful kids, the whole joy of living, and things that they may not be able to do now but have done before; how good it felt, how good it was.

When I'm with someone who is dying, I hold their hand, and sometimes, if they are conscious, they will say, "Thank you. It is okay." And I say, "Yes, it's okay. You have done your duty to mankind and to yourself. It's okay."

The other thing I really enjoy is having people around me and being able to encourage them. I always am a counselor to all my friends and try to let them know that whatever life is, it's okay to be unhappy, and it's okay to be happy, too.

What I celebrate about being a woman is the deep caring we have, not only for ourselves but for the other women around us. We are like lionesses. Lionesses take care of their cubs. They are not going to let anybody get around them. We will stand up with

that loving, that caring, that gentleness, and that awesome protective nature about us. That's why I wouldn't want to be anything but a woman. Nobody else can take a woman's place. Who but a woman can do what a woman does?

My advice is to be kind to just one person, to start taking care of each other and thinking about each other. And if one person can be like that, I think we could make the world a better place.

Marian

Marian (58) has raised two talented daughters and has a wide variety of creative activities and interests. After becoming a widow at a young age, she found her calling. She created and directs a caregiver center in a community hospital in New York, for which she has received national recognition.

My life has been a journey of self-exploration, learning to care for myself and like myself, to let my voice come through, and to trust that voice and my instincts. That inner voice has a lot to tell me. I have learned to trust my instincts a lot more than I used to.

I remember being very lonely as a child, sitting in the house by myself, waiting for somebody to come rescue me. I see that as a really vivid image. It makes me sad to think about it again. I felt so unsure of myself and so unsettled as to what my place in the universe was. That happens when you don't have that strong, early bonding with your mother. That's why mothers are so important and why it was so important to me to be a good mother.

There were a lot of "shoulds," "have tos," and "ought tos" in my life. It took a lot to overcome that sense of what other people were telling me to do, what I should do, and what I must do. I come back to this image of my own voice because it's what I see symbolically as being important to me—and to anyone: to be able to hear one's own voice and let that voice out.

I didn't have my daughters until I was in my late thirties. Part of it was because I didn't think I could be a good mother. I didn't think I wanted to be a mother. Now I really feel good about it, and

the relationship I have with them has been great. I can't imagine what my life would have been like if I didn't have my children. I've learned so much from them, and I've learned so much about myself by being a mother. I feel really good about how I was able to help them navigate through life. I hope I was a good role model for them.

Becoming a mother has been an opportunity for me to kind of retrieve the childhood I didn't have. What better thing could there be than to continue to learn about yourself and be able to be the best you that you can possibly be? That will always be my journey: to try to always be the best me that I can be. And, in the process, I am able to give more to other people and to share more of my happiness and joy.

If I think back about that little girl, and even who I was in my twenties, it's hard to recognize that person now. It was a long process of trying to find my voice. I went through many years of therapy, which really did help. A huge part of my journey was this self-exploration to understand why things happened in the past. You can't change them, but you can understand them and then move forward. You get a certain strength and resolve from that. So I say, "Okay, I wasn't dealt the best card in the deck, but I can do something about that."

A major challenge was seeing my husband become ill and die. Ken was so vital and so smart and capable—to just see him disappear before my eyes was hard. There was the grief and sadness of losing him when I was fifty-five. He died two days after my birthday. At times, I didn't really know if I could go on, if I could do this. I was amazed that I was able to find the strength to do it. Here was a situation that I was thrown into. I tapped into a pool and reservoir of strength and caring that I was amazed I had. I got up every day trying to make it through. I think, because I was able to handle Ken's dying in the way I did, it made it a little bit easier for my children. I feel empowered, having gotten through it, being able to do that for them.

I felt, after he died, that I had to do something to help other people, to take all the feelings I had and channel them in a way to make a difference in other people's lives. I created a caregiver center in Ken's memory. It is amazing! People come in and feel like a breath of fresh air has come into their lives. A calm sweeps over them, and, for a few minutes, it brings them some relief.

I need to start giving myself permission to take care of myself, just allow myself to have as much time for myself as I think I need. I still have this little sense of having to achieve, to do, to check things off. Taking care of myself is being with family and friends. I like to take walks and be out in nature. I do my best thinking when I'm by myself. I have learned to enjoy that time, even though I like to be with people. I also like to have massages and to exercise. I nurture myself that way because it's important for me. I feel fortunate that I've been able to really be introspective in my life and to celebrate and appreciate who I am. Sometimes it's hard to do that, to sort of take stock and say, "I'm okay; I'm a good person. I have my moments, but I guess we all do."

As I get older, I feel more joyous. There are so many wonderful things to enjoy. I love reading. I love pampering myself. I love music and art. Theater is wonderful. I love doing something physical. I love being out in nature and hiking and just communing with the beauty of it all. I love being with people. I love just having a great belly laugh. There are so many joyous things that life has to offer.

For me, what's great about being a woman, what I celebrate about being a woman, is that I can be both soft and strong. I love the fact that, as women, we can show emotions and we can have that soft, kind, gentle side. I love being able, at times, to be vulnerable and know it's okay. I know I don't always have to have all the answers and that I need other people.

Women are such good friends. I can get so much strength and comfort from other women. And I love being a woman; I love all the trappings that go with being a woman. I like the nice clothes

and being frilly at times and sexy and saucy and playing a lot of different roles.

We can be strong. We live in a day and age where that's acceptable in women. We can have opinions, and we can have our own voice. It's really exciting. We can make a difference. I think women really can be a voice of reason and openness because they will allow more in and perhaps don't have as much ego as men. I think it's wonderful that women are able to contribute that to the world. I'm really happy that I'm a woman.

My advice to other women is to embrace all the roles you play and to enjoy being those different sides of yourself. Be adaptable, go with the flow, and reinvent yourself. It's a little scary having to change gears, but it's so rewarding once you realize that you are able to do it, and that it's enriching.

I would say to young women, as I always say to my girls, "If nothing else, I really hope that you've learned to go with the flow. Handle things in a way that you are kind to yourself." Being kind to yourself is probably one of the most important gifts we can give ourselves.

Toby

Toby (56) has a PhD in environmental psychology and has written a book about design psychology that is used in programs throughout the country. She is a woman of tremendous creativity and resilience, having faced and come through many difficulties.

I come from a long line of strong, emotional Hungarian women with lots of *joie de vivre*. Women have the wonderful ability to connect with each other, support each other, see each other through the ups and downs, and be really steady. That is something I really cherish with my women friends.

In my journey through life, there have been a lot of ups and downs. My father got sick when I was two or three, had a second heart attack when I was thirteen, and died when I was sixteen.

My brother left home when he was sixteen and I was fourteen. I went through a divorce and then, recently, got breast cancer. Those are the downs. The ups were surviving all of those things and coming out a stronger person for having done so! I have had wonderful friendships and family members by my side. A lot of those friendships are with people who know me inside and out. That's really a special experience, a blessing.

As I think about my father's death and illness, I realize that nobody really talked it through or worked it through with me as a young person. I didn't have a way to come to grips with it. I think I was just muddling through and trying to become a human being.

What got me through the divorce were friends and family. Going into therapy, trying to understand my family origins and dynamics, and understanding how I could have a healthier time in the future really helped. My background—coming from women, like my mother, who were really strong and made it through whatever helped give me an identity as a strong person.

The biggest joy in my life is definitely my kids. Now they are nineteen and twenty-one, and they're doing well. They are wonderful people. They bring me a lot of joy, and that's a big thing. The friendships I have bring me a lot of joy, including friendships with my relatives. I feel like those are the really special things in my life that keep me going and mean a lot.

I always wanted to learn how to sail, and I finally did it. I like being out in the open. I like having this physical challenge where you have to be really *present*. You can't be thinking about or ruminating about anything or be into yourself when you're sailing. You have to be there, in the moment. It feels great. You are directing yourself against the elements.

I dealt with cancer by first melting down and crying and being hysterical and then being very businesslike about what I had to find out to get treated. I focused on things that made me feel creative and like I had some control of the situation. I found ways to use the experience to do something positive. I could sit around

and think that the cancer might come back, and I could get myself into a knot. Instead, I choose to say, "Okay, chances are it won't come back, so why waste this time? Enjoy your life." It's a little shadow that follows me, not a big cloud.

There is a great line: "My scars are the brushstrokes in the masterpiece that is my life." I think that we all experience wounds and scars, but that one line is fantastic. I think that's the way you have to frame it.

Unlike the losses and scars that you can't necessarily recoup (like the death of my father), there are some things that you can improve or change. In the case of my brother, I reconnected with him after not having seen him much for forty years. It wasn't that we were angry with each other; it's just that he lived in India, and I lived here. I spent two weeks with him in India, and we got to know each other. Even though there are many things we can't undo or change, there are things we can change, situations where "life comes around." That's really nice.

I started a field called "design psychology," which is the practice of architecture, planning, and interior design in which psychology is the principal tool. I help people design from within, thinking about who they are at the core and who they want to be. I then help them express that through colors, shapes, objects, furniture, and so on. I've written a book. It's been nourishing in my life, and it's something that I had to do, was inspired to do, wanted to do, and did!

My advice for women and their journeys through life is that it comes down to realizing your value in every way. Another piece of advice: When people don't value you, avoid them. It's really good if you can attune yourself to those people as best as possible. When you come across those who don't enhance your life, cut and run! Whether in a marriage, friendship, or working relationship, develop radar for that toxicity. So many people are absolutely the *opposite* of toxic. So many situations are *life-enhancing*. Why not gravitate toward those positive people and experiences?

The Elder Woman

An elder woman lives in a society that often isolates seniors, which sometimes leaves her lonely, yet she is full of life and savors a lifetime of wisdom. As she contemplates the tapestry of her life, she is challenged to maintain a sense of meaning and connectedness, as well as to cope with feelings about loss and aging.

Gloria

Gloria (84) had several careers, including teaching and interior design. She has found her niche lecturing to audiences in Florida, using book reviews and stories of her life that she has written. Gloria is the mother of Toby (midlife woman) and the grandmother of Sarah (young woman).

I had a pretty happy childhood with two parents who loved me. We didn't have much money, which was about par for the course because we were going through the Great Depression. I was Jewish in a non-Jewish community, which didn't bother me until the night my family was sitting in the living room and a rock came crashing through the window. The note attached to it, which said "Dirty Jew," was my first experience with discrimination. It hurt.

I was the first member of my clan to get a college education. You weren't expected to go to college, so getting a degree was a good feeling. I was fortunate to get a job teaching at the Women's College of Rutgers University during the war. I worked in the Speech Department for a year and then met my future husband and got married. That's what I was expected to do—get married and have children. It wasn't common for women to work outside the home. While my children were young, I wasn't happy just staying home with them. I found a way to express my creativity by working with community theater groups, writing and performing. These early loves stayed with me. I worked as an interior designer for about twenty years. It's almost like giving birth: you start with

125

an idea and a barren area, add some elements, make them come together, and suddenly there is the baby!

Now I am a professional book reviewer and storyteller, and I absolutely love doing it. I have to find the material, read it, decide what I want to say, and then go out and perform. I sometimes pinch myself to think that I am still commanding a salary and doing work I love.

My first husband, Nat, was ten years older than myself. I was still rather emotionally immature. He came along and was a "good catch" with an established business, so we did the traditional thing: we got married. We had two children, Toby and Jay. When we were married seven years, Nat had a catastrophic heart attack. For the next thirteen years of our marriage, he was ill and in and out of the hospital. He had another major coronary, which eventually proved fatal.

It was a very hard time for us all. I guess life, as you go through it, is made up of its share of losses. If you don't experience some sadness, if you don't let things touch you, you're probably not living a meaningful life. I've had losses that have touched me deeply. There was the death of my first husband and, later, the death of my second, whom I dearly loved during our twenty-three-year marriage.

My son, Jay, was a brilliant boy, caught up in the craziness of the sixties. Jay left home at seventeen. Then, when he was nineteen, Jay joined the Hare Krishna movement and became a Hindu. At first, that was overwhelming to me, so alien to everything I knew and understood. The change in Jay was dramatic. It was a difficult time. I was desperate to help him find his way back to "normal" (to attend college and start a career), but my husband, in his final illness, had a greater claim on my attention. I couldn't juggle both. I hoped that my son would become disenchanted with what seemed a crazy path. But he didn't. He immersed himself in the study of Hinduism. Seeing him wearing orange robes was very difficult for me, especially when people stared at him as if he were a freak.

126

All of these events threw me into a deep depression. I knew I had to get hold of myself and take control of my life again, and I went for help. My daughter depended on me, and I had to come to terms with my son. I had to try to accept his new life or lose him.

Jay went on to become a Hindu scholar, a book editor, and a very much loved and admired leader. I visited him in India, saw him in his own milieu, and realized that my son is a happy, fulfilled man, doing work that is important to him and to others. What better way to measure success?

I'm not normally a calm, quiet person. I'm Hungarian, after all, and tend to get emotional about things. When Jay comes to visit, though, he communicates an aura of serenity that stays with me for days.

My daughter, Toby, is a continuing joy in my life. She has two wonderful children, Liam and Sarah, and is an amazingly strong person. A smart lady with a delicious sense of humor, Toby is a can-do, will-do kind of woman, a great example of how to make lemonade out of lemons. She's had blows in her life I wish she hadn't suffered but that I couldn't prevent. I just try to be there for her. We share a particularly loving relationship that brings a special sweetness to my life.

I've learned a few lessons over the years. What happens is going to happen regardless of what you do. Maybe you can cry about it. Maybe it's even good to cry. In the end, though, you have to say, "This is what is on my plate. This is what has been dealt to me, and I have to get through another day in the best way I know how."

I've reached a stage in life where I'm comfortable with who I am. I'm more confident than I was as a younger person. I'm less judgmental. I have forgiven myself for the things I wish I had done differently. This is the essential me, and that's how it's going to be. I'm not about to undergo any seismic change at my age, although it's good to have an open mind.

Friends nurture me. That became increasingly important after I became a widow for the second time. I've been alone for twelve years now, and although I miss the warmth and love of a companion, friends help a lot.

I relish my independence. I like being in charge of what I do, where I go, who I am. I like quiet time and am perfectly happy to stay home with my own company.

I feel especially blessed that I'm able to work. I love reading, writing, and then performing the results of my efforts. My book reviews are a kind of performance since I draw on my early theatrical abilities to hold the interest of an audience. It's so affirming that I'm booked months in advance, and I'm still enough of a ham to enjoy a standing ovation now and then. I hope they're applauding the material and not the fact that I haven't keeled over yet.

I hope my health holds up and that I can continue what I'm doing. I can't imagine experiencing life without love and work. Love, of course, is love of family, nature, environment, whatever makes you feel good—even taking a nice hot bath—it's all a part of loving. Work is what gives me a sense of fulfillment and pleasure, that feeling of accomplishment. It's what makes my life complete.

Every day you start with a clean slate. You have the rare opportunity to make of it what you will. Write a new script. Consider possibilities. Make it work. It's your journey and your legacy.

Ray

Ray (100) was a lifelong teacher and continues to volunteer in local schools. She has a keen mind, is active in her community, and is always involved in helping others who need some assistance.

I can remember when I was three years old and lived in Poland, in a little town not too far from Warsaw. My father decided that America offered more for us, and so we all migrated here. I remember so clearly, even though I was so young, riding from our little home in this little village in a black carriage not unlike the

carriages the Amish people ride in. There was a little window in the back of the little carriage, and I turned around to look out the carriage and saw my tiny little grandmother standing there with her little white dog, waving her white handkerchief and stopping every once in a while to wipe her eyes. Many years later, we heard from our relatives in Poland that my grandmother died of a heart condition. I never believed it. I really believed she died of a broken heart from having her family move away from her. I know how I feel, having lost all my sisters, my only brother, my parents, beloved nephews, and so many, many people who were wonderful friends. I can see myself doing the same thing, standing somewhere and crying over the loss of those dear ones.

When I came to America, the first thing my father did was send me to school, and there I learned to speak English. My father went to night school and learned to read, write, and speak English. My mother could not speak English. She was busy with her six children and any stranger who had no place to stay. She was a wonderful, kind person like my grandmother was. I taught her to read and write English.

We were as poor as church mice. The older girls had to start working, in sweat shops of course. It was a poor home, but it was a home full of love. In spite of all the poverty, I remember nothing but happiness from all that time. For a penny, you could get a half of a penny's worth of this or a half penny's worth of that at a candy store. My sisters once put their little pennies together and bought me the only toy I ever had, which was a doll with a china face and blonde hair. I carried her around with me all the time. We had enough. We had enough! What wonderful times. Our games were very simple. We played Stoop Ball: we would throw a ball against the steps of the stoop and then catch it. We played Double Dutch Rope. I had lots of friends. My brother was just a little over a year older than I am. He and I went to school together. I remember in the winter the homeowners would shovel the snow away from their sidewalks and pile it up in a high pile outside. Of course, the winters were cold, and so the snow piles turned pretty hard, and

my brother and I used to walk on top of the snow piles, sixteen blocks to school. This was in Brooklyn, New York.

I was thinking about writing a little piece about the vehicles in my life. It started with a horse and buggy, and then a horse and wagon if you were doing something like carting vegetables or being a peddler, and then they had electric street cars where they had an arm that attached itself to the overhead electric wires. Then we had street cars with a running board. In the summer time, we'd hang on the outside; we'd stand on the running board and hold on to the bars and ride along to the beach or wherever we were going. I can remember when we had gas mantels. First, it was oil lamps, and then it was gas. We lived near stables with horses in them. The milk wagon came by, distributed the milk, and left it by our doorstep.

I had so little when I was young; I was very appreciative of everything I had. A penny was a lot. Movies were two for five cents. And if you had three cents, you looked for somebody who had two cents, and we'd go to the movies and see it twice, of course.

I have so many memories. It's wonderful living to my age and having all these memories. I have lived through so much; the First World War, the Second World War. I remember buying savings stamps during the First World War for twenty-five cents, and we pasted them in a book.

The challenges I had as an adult were the illnesses of my husband. He had thirteen operations in his lifetime, some of them extremely serious: brain surgery, a colon operation for cancer. He survived all of it. He was a tall, well-structured, healthy person. He was very brave and almost a daring person. If the doctor said "operation," he said, "When do we go?"

I am a strong person. People say, "In an emergency, call Ray." When I was teaching, I was in charge of accidents in the school. Nobody else could handle a child being run over by a car or something like that. When I'm needed, I'm there. Later on, I feel it and stop to become emotional about it. But when I'm needed, I gather strength from something, I don't know what it is.

I say without modesty that the thing that gives me pleasure is being able to do for others. I should be thanking them for the opportunity to give to me the wonderful feeling that I am able, even at my age now, to do some little thing for someone, even if it is just opening a door for a woman who has a walker. I've learned in life to take care of myself mentally, physically, and medically so that I will not be a burden to my children. I have enjoyed excellent health through all my many years and hope to go on for another few years doing what I'm doing now.

One way I take care of myself is by eating sensibly. I think of my early childhood, the food we had was plucked from the garden. It was all fresh, all the vitamins were there. We didn't know we were eating healthy. We just ate it because we enjoyed it. I don't eat too much. I have three to four meals a day: a little breakfast, a little lunch, a little dinner, a little snack at night before I go to bed. I am a good patient. I do what the doctor tells me to do. I read a lot. I do crossword puzzles, especially the *New York Times*, because I enjoy doing that. I properly take my meds. I enjoy walking, doing the exercises now that I can do, which is just walking up and down the hallway. I was very active in sports. I played basketball, tennis, golf, and soccer in high school. When I wasn't engaged in a sport, I was a cheerleader for the team.

I would certainly tell every woman to have some goal, some ambition, something that is a service to yourself, to your family, to your country. That's tops. That's number one. Go out and do what you are capable of doing. Get yourself involved; keep your mind open. Nurture yourself first because, if you don't, you can't nurture someone else. Then do something for someone else. It really uplifts you; it really is a fullness, a feeling that you get knowing that you did something. Don't expect a "thanks" because the thanks should be coming from your side that they gave you the opportunity to do something that makes you feel so good.

Absolutely be good to yourself. Do for others; be there for each other; be good to each other; be kind to each other.

Celebration and Advice

We asked all of the women we interviewed what they celebrate about women and also what advice they would give to other women. Many of those wise and delicious words are included in the preceding section, but we want you to have the benefit of sharing the celebration and advice that each woman has to share with you, even if we couldn't include her full story.

Marge, mid-nineties, retired psychiatrist

I think there is something very special about women. In my experience, women have been so much easier to talk to and find it so much easier to express themselves. They *love* to talk to each other and can be easily more intimate with other people. Women want to know how relationships work. With a good woman friend, you can be so much more intimate.

My advice to other women is to keep busy, have intimate relationships, love, and work. Find things to do that interest you. Fight for your rights. Be strong! Fight for what you want! I admire this kind of strength. I would advise women not to withdraw but be strong. If you go to a party and you don't know a soul, go up to someone and say, "My name is this and I do that and what is your name?" Be socially aggressive as well as career aggressive.

Danute, early seventies, dancer and artist

I celebrate women. There is a sisterhood. There are just some women that I feel really comfortable and close with, and it feels good. It is a totally different relationship than with the guys. It's more intimate.

My advice for other women is to have interests. If something interests you, go for it. I was lucky that I had interests when I became alone. I had dance class, I had tennis, and I loved to read. Those things didn't leave me shut up in the house. I had actual schedules to attend to, and I would see people. There were good relationships associated with those activities.

Susan, midsixties, social worker and retreat leader

I like that nurturing sense of compassion that women have. I celebrate that. I've always valued that sense of being close to somebody and almost having them finish your sentences, understanding. That's been good.

I would like to tell women that we are never limited. We really aren't. There's no reason to give up on a hope or a dream. It may need to be tabled, but that doesn't mean it won't come back if it has some juice. The other thing I've learned is that if you take a step in any direction, things will come towards you. Once you have said "I'm going to do this little thing" and you are willing, other things present themselves. Invitations start to come when you say yes to something. You are not in it all alone and struggling all by yourself.

Karen, midsixties, retired special education teacher

I celebrate many, many things about being a woman. I am so glad to be a woman. I value so much the quality of being there for another, taking the time and the energy for just listening and sharing. And being able to slow down when life gets too fast. I value our being able to ask for help when we need it. We reach out to each other. I like supporting each other, helping each other. I celebrate our ability to share with each other, to model how we live our lives to each other. I think we learn so much by being together.

I'd like other women to not be afraid to keep growing and changing. When you retire, don't put a lid on your life. I have a sense there's so much more. Find your passions, and go with them. Take the time to clear away the clutter in your life. It's okay to spend time alone; definitely okay to say "no" to others. Be confident in your choices, and don't be afraid to change your mind or your direction.

Tanya, midsixties, real estate agent and grandmother

I celebrate other women—their openness, their confidentiality. They understand confidences. They share so much: women's beauty, their insight, their laughter, long friendships that have been easy and wonderful.

I'd like other women to know about their boundaries and their rights. I didn't even know how important my boundaries were until I was almost fifty years old. I want women to understand that they are vulnerable in ways that most men are not vulnerable. Whether they learn self-defense, are athletes, or strong, capable corporate women, they are vulnerable. A woman could stand up and say, "I need to know a little bit more, please, before I can say yes." I want women to know how to name and honor their feelings.

Lena, midfifties, home health aide for seniors

I am proud to be a woman. I have lots of nice friends that are very good to me. We are good to each other. We share our sorrows and our joys with each other and comfort each other.

If I had advice to give other women, I would say have a lot of love in you. Be kind.

Love and respect yourself; respect others. Love yourself; love others. That will take you through. You have to have a sense of forgiveness. Sometimes it's very hard when other people ridicule you. Keep forgiving and let go and don't hate. That's how I get my strength. I am a strong person. I learn to accept what comes. In whatever position I'm in, I just learn to be content.

Leah, midfifties, college teacher of gender studies, musician

What I can celebrate about being a woman is friendship and companionship. I still feel like the bottom line is that I can celebrate the kind of woman that I am. I know society doesn't really. So I have to have a little private celebration. I think being a

woman can give you a good critical outsider's perspective on social institutions. There is a real advantage to that. That's what Virginia Woolf always talked about. We are members of the outsiders' society. We can be. I strongly celebrate that.

Advice? Don't be afraid to be vulnerable and look awkward. Be willing to start over again. You have to be like a snake and lose your skin. There's a lot of vulnerability and awkwardness in that process. Growth is all about vulnerability and awkwardness. If you are not feeling those things, then you are not growing. I definitely think that's important.

Mary, early twenties, working in dramatic arts with children in Africa and in New York

It's a woman's time. I'm really grateful that we can see things differently and come into our full potential as women and as people on the planet. Going, doing, being powerful are all okay.

What advice do I have for other women? The biggest thing I would say is that nobody has it all together. Nobody feels like they have all the answers. You just have to go with what you're feeling. That's what's going to make you happy. If you make yourself do something and you don't want to do it or you let someone else convince you to do it, you are just going to be unhappy. You have to do what makes you happy. You have to trust yourself.

Josie, seventeen, senior in high school

I celebrate girl power. It's a force. It's silly when women try to be like men. Yes, I'm not able to lift things, but I can do a lot of things.

I would like women my age to know they don't have to put way so much focus on other people's impressions of them. Really trust people, and don't shield yourself too much. Take care of yourself. Exercise, even if you have a lot of homework. Eat well. Take care of yourself.

The interviews were such a wonderful part of the process of writing this book that we want to encourage you to participate by answering the interview questions for yourself (see Journal Reflections in "Shine Like the Sun"). You could also interview friends or use the questions to share your life stories in a group. And if you want to take it a step further, sit down and interview a woman who is not in your life stage or of your background, career path, religion, or hometown. You will be touched, as we were, by the strength and wisdom, by your similarities, and by the wonderful spirit of woman that comes through each of us. We will post interviews our readers send to us on our website: www.StandFlowShine.com.

More Resources for Your Self-Care Journey

We recommend these books, CDs, and DVDs to strengthen and expand your self-care journey.

Self-Care

Jean Shinoda Bolen. *The Millionth Circle: How to Change Ourselves and the World – The Essential Guide to Women's Circles.* Conari Press.

Joan Z. Boryzenko. *Inner Peace for Busy Women: Balancing Work, Family, and Your Inner Life.* Hay House.

Joan Z. Boryzenko. *A Woman's Book of Life.* Riverhead Trade.

Boston Women's Health Book Collective and Judy Norsigian. *Our Bodies, Ourselves.* Touchstone.

Harvard Women's Health Watch – Trusted Advice for a Healthier Life. Harvard Health Publications. (a monthly publication)

Kristin Neff. *Self-Compassion: Stop Beating Yourself Up and Leave Insecurity Behind.* Harper Collins.

Christiane Northrup. *Women's Bodies, Women's Wisdom: Creating Physical and Emotional Health and Healing.* Revised edition. Bantam.

Linda Breen Pierce. *Simplicity Lessons: A 12-Step Guide to Living Simply.* Gallagher Press.

Julie K. Silver. *You Can Heal Yourself: A Guide to Physical and Emotional Recovery After Injury or Illness.* St. Martin's Paperbacks.

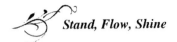

Stand, Flow, Shine

Body Movement

Donna Farhi. *The Breathing Book: Vitality and Good Health through Essential Breath Work.* Holt.

Donna Farhi. *Yoga Mind, Body and Spirit: A Return to Wellness.* Holt.

Judith Hanson Lasater. *Relax and Renew: Restful Yoga for Stressful Times.* Rodmell Press.

Daisy Lee. *Daisy Lee's Radiant Lotus Qigong* DVDs and YouTube videos. (any of her videos; start with her Talk)

Patricia Kerr Meera. *Big Yoga: A Simple Guide for Bigger Bodies.* Square One.

Linda Sparrow, Patricia Walden, and Judith Hanson Lasater. *The Woman's Book of Yoga and Health: A Lifelong Guide to Wellness.* Shambhala.

Creativity

Julia Cameron. *The Artist's Way.* Jeremy P. Tarcher/Putnam.

Susanne Fincher. *Coloring Mandalas.* Shambhala. (all volumes)

Susanne Fincher. *The Mandala Workbook: A Creative Guide for Self-Exploration, Balance, and Well-Being.* Shambhala.

Toby Israel. *Some Place Like Home: Using Design Psychology to Create Ideal Places.* Design Psychology Press.

Jan Phillips. *Marry Your Muse: Making a Lasting Commitment to Your Creativity.* Quest Books.

Meditation

Pema Chodron. *Start Where You Are.* Shambhala.

Thich Nhat Hanh. *Making Space: Creating a Home Meditation Practice.* Parallax Press.

Thich Nhat Hanh. *Peace Is Every Step: The Path of Mindfulness in Everyday Life.* Bantam Books.

Sharon Salzberg. *Real Happiness: The Power of Meditation, A 28-Day Program.* Workman Publishing.

Journal Writing

Carolyn G Heilbrun. *Writing a Woman's Life*. W.W. Norton and Company.

Samara O'Shea. *Note to Self: On Keeping a Journal and Other Dangerous Pursuits*. William Morris Press.

Take on a Retreat

Aliki Barnstone, ed. *The Shambhala Anthology of Women's Spiritual Poetry*. Shambhala.

Sylvia Boorstein. *Happiness Is an Inside Job: Practicing for a Joyful Life*. Ballantine Books.

Anne Morrow Lindberg. *Gift from the Sea*. Pantheon Books.

Jennifer Louden. *The Woman's Retreat Book: A Guide to Restoring, Rediscovering, and Reawakening Your True Self in a Moment, an Hour, a Day, or a Weekend*. Harper San Francisco.

Any poetry by Mary Oliver, Alice Walker, Emily Dickinson, Lucille Clifton, Denise Levertov, Ursula LeGuin.

Games

New Games Foundation, *The New Games Book*. Main Street Books.

Matthew Toone. *Great Games! 175 Games and Activities for Families, Groups, and Children*. Mullerhaus Publishing Arts, Inc.

Additional Resources on Women's Journeys

Mary Catherine Bateson. *Composing a Life*. Plume Paperbacks.

Clarissa Pinkola Estes. *Women Who Run with the Wolves*. Balantine Books.

Susanne Fincher. *Menopause: The Inner Journey*. Shambhala.

Lucky Sweeny, Bonnie Kelley, Andrea Hylen, and Karen Porter, eds. *Conscious Choices: An Evolutionary Woman's Guide to Life*.

Who We Are

Judith:

   I have many wonderful years of experience as a psychotherapist, workshop and retreat leader, and national trainer for workshop facilitation. I am so happy to lead Women's Wisdom Journeys and Stand, Flow, Shine Workshops. My joys are nurturing and empowering women, using our inherent wisdom for health and healing, and finding peace within. I love sharing self-care processes with other women, both in Maryland and in the Northwest.

Marilyn:

   I am a licensed counselor and a trainer and facilitator of the Bonny Method of Guided Imagery and Music. My work is focused in the field of holistic healing and therapy. I believe that with a little encouragement women can learn to make time for themselves in their busy lives. I love helping women identify their strengths, express their creativity, and experience moments of pure joy. I live in Baltimore where I have a private practice and enjoy storytelling and writing.

Find out more about the authors and the Stand, Flow, Shine
workshops at www.StandFlowShine.com

CPSIA information can be obtained at www.ICGtesting.com
Printed in the USA
BVOW07s1057260813

329391BV00001B/5/P